CHRISTMAS COMES

YOUR GUIDE TO A GREAT CHRISTMAS

JACKIE ALLEN

CHRISTMAS COMES
Published by Kopi Books
105B 5555 Youngstown Warren Road
Niles, OH 44446 U.S.A.

Unless otherwise noted, all Scripture quotations are taken from the Holman Christian Standard Bible® Copyright © 1999, 2000, 2002, 2003 by Holman Bible Publishers. Used by permission. Holman Christian Standard Bible®, Holman CSB®, and HCSB® are federally registered trademarks of Holman Bible Publishers.

Scripture quotations marked CSB have been taken from the Christian Standard Bible®, Copyright © 2017 by Holman Bible Publishers. Used by permission. Christian Standard Bible® and CSB® are federally registered trademarks of Holman Bible Publishers.

Scripture quotations marked NIV are from the Holy Bible, New International Version®, NIV® Copyright © 1973, 1978, 1984, 2011 by Biblica, Inc.® Used by permission. All rights reserved worldwide.

Scripture quotations are from the ESV® Bible (The Holy Bible, English Standard Version®), Copyright © 2001 by Crossway, a publishing ministry of Good News Publishers. Used by permission. All rights reserved.

Scripture quotations taken from the 21st Century King James Version®, copyright © 1994. Used by permission of Deuel Enterprises, Inc., Gary, SD 57237. All rights reserved.

ISBN 978-0-578-97986-1
Copyright © 2021 by Jackie Allen
Design: Lydia Tarleton
Printed in the United States of America 2021

Jackie Allen has done it again. His newest book, *Christmas Comes*, is not only perfectly written, but it perfectly captures the heart and spirit of Christmas. Biblical insight, inspiring stories, practical action steps, and even a touch of humor make this book a must-read for everyone. I STRONGLY encourage you to grab a few copies. Get it in the hands of your family and friends, and let it serve as a launching pad to reunite you and those around you to the true meaning of this historical celebration. You won't be disappointed!

CHRIS SONKSEN
Founder of Church Boom
Author

This book is dedicated to my parents, Paul and Peggy, who always worked to make Christmas a special time for me and my sister growing up. Merry Christmas, Mom and Dad!

TABLE OF CONTENTS

FOREWORD

BY ANDREW BAILEY

One of my fondest childhood memories took place on Christmas morning when I was six years old. All of the presents were wrapped and stuffed under the tree. Meanwhile, my brothers and I were waiting in anticipation to tear off the paper and see what gifts fate had brought us.

We started with the stockings then moved to the smaller presents we were obligated to open. Finally, a box that was about four feet long by three feet wide was placed in front of me. I had no idea what it was, and my excitement levels were running through the roof.

Somehow, being the youngest of three boys, my wish list was non-existent that year. Christmas at our house was more about managing the chaos of the season than giving and receiving extravagant gifts. My parents had their hands full just making sure we brothers didn't beat each other up. I came to Christmas as a bright-eyed, bushy-tailed six-year-old with no expectations and no longings. But before I knew it, I was sitting in front of a huge box with my name on it. As I tore back the layers of wrapping paper, my interest was piqued by the Star Wars logo on the top left corner of the box. My adrenaline increased as I ripped the last piece of paper off, and there it was in all of its glory—an action figure-sized X-Wing.

My eyes lit up and my jaw dropped. I was so caught off guard. I didn't ask for any gifts and didn't even know I wanted them. But at that moment, nothing brought me more joy than that X-Wing that was bigger than my head. As a bonus, it came with a Luke Skywalker action figure to pilot the starfighter for all of my future battles.

To this day, I still have that X-Wing and Luke Skywalker sitting in a plastic tub, waiting for my kids to get old enough to appreciate them. As I look back on that Christmas, what made that moment so great was that I had zero expectations. I knew gifts would come, but somehow, *that* gift at *that* time blew away any dream of what I thought Christmas could be.

My friend, mentor, and pastor Jackie Allen's new book, *Christmas Comes*, ignites the same emotions I felt on that Christmas during my childhood. Often, we are not ready for Christmas to come, or we are prepared to reject it when it arrives. But that still doesn't change the spiritual, historical, and personal impact of the truth that Christmas comes.

It comes every year, but not as some new or reinvented form of Christmas. It arrives as a remembrance and reflection of the spiritual coming of Jesus into our lives. We can try to ignore it, but it relentlessly knocks on the door of our hearts whether we like it or not. We can choose to approach the holiday season with grumpiness and disdain, or with a childlike innocence, ready to embrace the gift of Christmas.

Just like Christmas surprised me during my childhood, it can also create a sense of awe and wonder in you. Reading this book with fresh eyes, an open mind, and a soft heart will help you experience your best Christmas yet. So, let me give you some direction on how to use the three sections of *Christmas Comes*:

THE MAIN CONTENT

This is the heart of the book. Ultimately, it proves the case of how unavoidable Christmas and Jesus really are. For the pastor, the church-goer, and the skeptic, Jackie lays out the true meaning of Christmas in a thought-provoking way. He challenges us not to breeze past it like any other day but to allow it to impact us personally.

THE ADVENT DEVOTIONAL

Ultimately, the goal of this book is to point you to Jesus and help you grow closer to Him. There is no better way to do that than by reading and reflecting on God's words, the Bible. That's why we prepared a daily Advent Devotional for you to read every day this Christmas Season. Each day includes different scriptures to read, as well as reflection questions that you can answer for yourself or with family and friends.

THE CHURCH RESOURCES

If you are a pastor or ministry leader, Jackie's heart is for *Christmas Comes* to be a resource that draws your church and community closer to God's heart this Christmas. Free sermon outlines, teachings, and graphics surrounding the four major themes of this book can be accessed and used to bless your church. The sermons and content are centered around these four main ideas from the book:

- Christmas Comes: The Gift of Christmas
- Christmas Comes: The Thieves of Christmas
- Christmas Comes: The Love of Christmas
- Christmas Comes: The Result of Christmas

I know many churches will be drawn deeper into a relationship with Jesus from these resources, and I am confident that some will say "Yes" to Jesus for the first time. Furthermore, I know that you will be drawn deeper into your walk with Him as you learn His true heart this Christmas. I recommend that you devour this book and its resources, and take in the great joy that Jesus wants to bring you through it.

ANDREW BAILEY
Cross Church Campus Pastor / Phoenix AZ

INTRODUCTION

CHRISTMAS COMES

Christmas comes!

One of our family's favorite Christmas memories is a classic yearly saying from my wife's grandmother. Every year on Christmas day she'd say the exact same thing. It was after all the presents were unwrapped, the paper was thrown all over the place, and the kids had stopped playing with their new toys and moved on to the boxes. That's when Grandma would walk into the room, smile, and say: "Christmas comes but once a year, and when it comes, it brings great cheer."

Think about the first two words of grandma's saying: *Christmas comes*. For some of us, the coming of Christmas each year brings more fear than cheer—more stressing than blessing. As a pastor, I have to be honest and say that for years I dreaded Christmas for multiple reasons. Buying gifts for the kids and family always put stress on our personal finances. And between Christmas programs, parties, and extra services at the church, there was a lot to plan and prepare for. I'm on record for jokingly saying that Christmas is my sixth favorite holiday. At one point, it got so bad that my family and church staff would lovingly call me the Grinch. At least I hope that it was lovingly?

Maybe Christmas is a magical time of the year for you, filled with stress-free generosity, unburdensome events, and quality time with a tension-free family. If that's the case, I'm happy for you! But maybe, just maybe, you feel the same way about Christmas that I have in the past. Am I the only one who gets a little *grinchy* around Christmas?

One of my favorite Christmas movies is the Tim Allen flick titled *Christmas with the Kranks*. It is based on a book called *Skipping Christmas* by John Grisham. In case you haven't seen it, I'll give you a synopsis (spoiler alert!). The plot centers around two empty-nesters, Luther and Nora Krank, who planned to skip out on the usual holiday festivities and sneak off for a Caribbean vacation. Imagine a year without Christmas: no crowded malls, no corny office parties, no fruitcakes, and no unwanted presents. That's the type of fantasy that Luther and Nora had in mind when they decided, just this once, they'd skip the holiday altogether. They'd be the only house on Hemlock Street without a rooftop Frosty or a Christmas tree. They figured that they wouldn't need either of those things, as their Caribbean cruise would set sail on Christmas Day. They even had the nerve to cancel their annual neighborhood party on Christmas Eve, leaving the neighbors distraught. But, as this weary couple discovered, skipping Christmas isn't half as easy as you'd imagine. In fact, it brings enormous consequences.

The Kranks couldn't skip Christmas, and, as badly as we may want to at times, we can't avoid Christmas, either. The point is that Christmas comes. It comes whether we want it to or not. It comes whether we are ready for it or not. It comes whether we like it or not.

Now, let's expand our perspective of the holiday. Think about Christmas from a larger viewpoint—the *real Christmas*—not the Christmas of our culture but the Christmas of Scripture. The real Christmas came with an inexplicable and inevitable force. What do I mean? Nothing could stop it: not King Herod, not all the powers of Rome, not the prideful Pharisees, and not the difficulties of excessive taxation and travel. Christmas came with the force and stealth-like accuracy of a Navy SEAL team on a top-secret mission.

Here's the inevitable, unshakable, and unchangeable truth: Christmas comes! In the Bible, we know that Christmas came with authority and power. It came with purpose and precision. It arrived with love and grace. When Christmas showed up on the scene, suddenly, the world became a better place. It brought hope where there was hopelessness and light where there was darkness.

One of my favorite things to do every Christmas is reciting the Christmas story from memory. In my opinion, there isn't a more powerful and poetic passage in the entire world. Let's start our Christmas journey by reading this passage together:

In those days Caesar Augustus issued a decree that a census should be taken of the entire Roman world. (This was the first census that took place while Quirinius was governor of Syria.) And everyone went to their own town to register.

So Joseph also went up from the town of Nazareth in Galilee to Judea, to Bethlehem the town of David, because he belonged to the house and line of David. He went there to register with Mary, who was pledged to be married to him and was expecting a child. While they were there, the time came for the baby to be born, and she gave birth to her firstborn, a son. She wrapped him in cloths and placed him in a manger, because there was no guest room available for them.

And there were shepherds living out in the fields nearby, keeping watch over their flocks at night. An angel of the Lord appeared to them, and the glory of the Lord shone around them, and they were terrified. But the angel said to them, "Do not be afraid. I bring you good news that will cause great joy for all the people. Today in the town of David a Savior has been born to you; he is the Messiah, the Lord. This will be a sign to you: You will find a baby wrapped in cloths and lying in a manger."

Suddenly a great company of the heavenly host appeared with the angel, praising God and saying,

> *"Glory to God in the highest heaven,*
> *and on earth peace to those on whom his favor rests."*

When the angels had left them and gone into heaven, the shepherds said to one another, "Let's go to Bethlehem and see this thing that has happened, which the Lord has told us about."

So they hurried off and found Mary and Joseph, and the baby, who was lying in the manger. When they had seen him, they spread the word concerning what had been told to them about this child, and all who heard it were amazed at what the shepherds said to them. But Mary treasured up all these things and pondered them in her heart. The shepherds returned, glorifying and praising God for all the things they had heard and seen, which were just as they had been told. (Luke 2:1-20, NIV)

Yes, indeed, Christmas comes. The purpose of this little book is to help prepare you and your family's hearts for Christmas. My hope is that it will change your outlook on Christmas, from drudgery to joy, the same way mine has been transformed over the years. I pray that you will be able to see past the cultural trimmings of Christmas and instead discover the real meaning and hope packed inside of it. The whole point of this book is to point you to *THE BOOK* this holiday season. When you flip to the back, you'll discover a Scripture reading and devotional plan to help guide your family through this season.

Let's make this Christmas about rich worship and deep appreciation for the one who came on the first Christmas, bringing peace and joy to the entire world. Let's get ready because, like it or not, Christmas is coming! And this year it's going to change everything.

CHAPTER 1

CHRISTMAS COMES UNEXPECTEDLY

One of the unusual things about Christmas is that it sometimes shows up in unexpected ways. As crazy as it may sound, it can sometimes catch us by surprise. Who doesn't like a little Christmas surprise?

As we find out from her short story in *Chicken Soup for the Soul: It's Christmas!,* Heather Thompson certainly loved Christmas surprises. Heather lived in Canada but orchestrated an elaborate Christmas surprise for her sister, who lived in Australia and was graduating from college there. Here's her recollection of her family's special moment:

> "For me, Christmas surprises are epitomized by presents. Or at least boxes. What if I could arrive at my sister's house unexpected for Christmas in a box? I started to plot. Then, brilliance struck. Getting delivered in a box to my sister's house by couriers! I knew if I pulled this off, my presence at her graduation and my grand arrival would be the best Christmas present I could ever give my sister. No one appreciates a prank like a prankster!
>
> Although I was leaving in less than seventy-two hours, I frantically jumped on my computer in Halifax, Nova Scotia, Canada, and started Googling courier companies. One of the first I came across, and the only one willing to go along with my Christmas surprise, was CouriersPlease. At first the branch manager said no, pointing out that Christmas was their busiest season and he couldn't spare a courier for this rather unorthodox request. But he suddenly and inexplicably warmed up to the idea and actually volunteered to dress up and deliver me himself. The Christmas Spirit strikes again!
>
> Upon arrival in Australia, the manager met me in full uniform, but that wasn't all. He'd brought one of his couriers, plus a

CouriersPlease van along for the ride as well! They even had a reinforced box prepared for me that they'd already tested at the office. I'd thought it would be easiest to walk up to the doorway, and then jump in the box while they rang the doorbell. But no, they insisted; my sister might see me through the window and they certainly didn't want to jeopardize my Christmas surprise. Instead, they parked a few hundred meters up the street, where they loaded me in the box and carried me all the way up to my sister's, where they rang the doorbell and announced they had a delivery for her.

I couldn't see the look on my sister's face as she opened the door to couriers with a surprise delivery, but I could tell from her voice that she was more than a little perplexed. This soon morphed into utter disbelief and shock when the box was opened and she saw her older sister sitting inside smiling up at her. She was at a complete loss for words, and I will never forget the look on her face as she opened those flaps on the box.

It was such a gift to be able to attend my sister's graduation, and to show her my love by giving her the most unique, unconventional Christmas present in the history of our family. It was a memory both she and I will cherish forever. It also served as a lesson for me: never, ever underestimate the power of the Christmas Spirit. It can move hearts, minds, and yes, even people in boxes."[1]

Imagine someone showing up for Christmas at your house, unannounced, in a beautifully wrapped box. What an amazing and totally unexpected surprise that would be!

Ironically, the arrival of Jesus on that first Christmas wasn't all that different. But instead of wrapping Himself in a box, the Son of God wrapped Himself in human flesh and came to live among us for thirty-three years. The Apostle Paul would explain it this way in the book of Philippians:

> *Who, being in very nature God, did not consider equality with God something to be used to his own advantage; rather, he made himself nothing by taking the very nature of a servant being made in human likeness. And being found in appearance as a man, he humbled himself by becoming obedient to death—even death on a cross!* (Philippians 2:6-8, NIV)

The Apostle John used even more mystical language in his description of Jesus' arrival:

> *In the beginning was the Word, and the Word was with God, and the Word was God. He was with God in the beginning.* (John 1:1-2, NIV)

> *The Word became flesh and made his dwelling among us. We have seen his glory, the glory of the one and only Son, who came from the Father, full of grace and truth.* (John 1:14, NIV)

What a gloriously wrapped present Jesus was that first Christmas. But as glorious as He was, and still is, I bet that His coming was a major surprise. In other words, the first Christmas came unexpectedly!

Think about it. No one was really expecting Jesus to come at the time that He did. You might be thinking, *But what about those who came to visit? My nativity scene would suggest otherwise!* Yes, some wise men were looking for Him—but let's be real, they showed up nearly two years late. The shepherds found baby Jesus more quickly, but the only reason He was on their radar in the first place was because the angel first found them in a nearby field. The innkeeper didn't even bother to make room for Jesus in his own establishment. Heck, His coming was even a massive surprise to Mary and Joseph, His own parents, some nine months earlier. When Mary, who was a virgin, found out she was pregnant with the Messiah, her first response was, "How can this be…?" (Luke 1:34, NIV). The first Christmas even caught Jesus' own mother by surprise!

Honestly, why would anybody be looking for Jesus to come? At the end of the Old Testament, God spoke through his prophet Malachi and then didn't speak again until the events of the New Testament. Bible scholars refer to this gap in Scripture as the intertestamental period, and it lasted for 400 years. That's 400 years of complete silence from God. It's hard to even imagine! For His people, who had seen His miracles firsthand, it probably felt like an eternity. And the longer that God was silent, the worse things became within their society. It seemed as if God had forgotten about both His people and the promises that He had made to them.

I'm sure that God's people had many questions like: "God, have you forgotten about all Your promises and predictions that you spoke through the prophets in the Old Testament? Will you ever speak to us again? Why, God, are you so quiet?"

These all would have been honest questions for people living during this era. Yet, we now know that God was working during the silence to bring us the Savior of the world.

It begs questions in our lives as Christians today: Is God ever silent in your life? Does it seem like He is sometimes aloof? Can you relate to those living amid 400 years of God's perceived inactivity?

Unfortunately, when God goes silent, it doesn't take long until we assume that He must have forgotten about us. Suddenly, we begin to take matters into our own hands—walking away from God in the process. But here's some encouragement: A waiting season is never a wasted season. God always works while we wait. Waiting always does significant work inside of us and it reminds us who is in control and prepares us for what's next.

A WAITING SEASON IS NEVER A WASTED SEASON. GOD ALWAYS WORKS WHILE WE WAIT.

This concept of waiting reminds me of a man named Simeon in Luke chapter two. Simeon was a great man of faith who lived through some of God's extended time of silence. Having suffered the oppression of God's people, he heard over and over again about how God had abandoned and forgotten them. As a result, he had watched many fall away in hopelessness and despair.

However, in the middle of the hopelessness of God's people, Simeon clung to hope from a promise that God had made him. The Bible says, "It had been revealed to him by the Holy Spirit that he would not die before he had seen the Lord's Messiah" (Luke 2:26, NIV). Simeon, one of the only people who was actually expecting the arrival of Jesus, faithfully clung to the promises of God, believing that He would come through in the end. And ultimately, God did! Imagine Simeon's joy to be one of the first people to hold the Messiah in his arms, experiencing firsthand the promise of God revealed!

Are you in the midst of a season of waiting? Maybe it has been a very long and incredibly frustrating few months or years. You might feel as though God has forgotten you and you're beginning to doubt. Whatever you do, don't lose hope—God is at work in the waiting. Even during the most challenging seasons, God wants to point us to Jesus. Jesus, the only one who can perfectly and completely fulfill the deepest longings of our hearts.

In Auschwitz, on one of the walls in the concentration camps of World War II, there's a powerful inscription that was carved by one of the prisoners of war. It reads: "I believe in the sun when it doesn't shine…I believe in the moon when I cannot see it…and I believe in God even when He is silent."

When it seems like the sun and moon aren't shining, and God is not speaking—hold on to hope. And if you're seeking hope—look to Jesus. If you need comfort—look to Jesus. If you're feeling unfulfilled and dissatisfied—look to Jesus. Jesus is the ultimate source of hope and joy, even when it feels like you're waiting on Him for 400 years.

THE FULLNESS OF TIME

The point is that Christmas surprised the world. And when you look at the Bible in its entirety, you will discover that Jesus has a habit of showing up at just the right time. He is never early and He is never late. That's true of His coming at Christmas, His arrival throughout history, and how He shows up in your life.

Paul said this of Jesus' arrival: "But when the fullness of the time was come, God sent forth his Son, made of a woman, made under the law" (Galatians 4:4, KJ21). What did he mean when he wrote the *fullness of time*?

Long before Jesus' birth, God was already preparing the way. There are two genealogies in the Gospels that show us the family line of Jesus. They take us back in time and show us that Jesus' origins trace back to the beginning of the human race in Adam (Luke 3:23-27), and the beginning of Israel through Abraham and David (Matthew 1:1–17). God was preparing the way centuries before the birth of His Son in Bethlehem.

You might be wondering, *How did God prepare the way?* Since God rules over human history, He undoubtedly shaped the history of the nations. The dominance of the Roman Empire had an impact on Israel—the context that Jesus was born into—and the spread of the Gospel by the early Christian church. Certainly, this was a part of God's preparation—He used the history of the nations to achieve His purposes.

However, in Scripture *the fullness of time* also points us in a different direction. Here, the *fullness of time* is defined by the unfulfilled promises that God had given to Old Testament Israel—ones filled with hope for future blessing and peace. As His people waited, God had already set a time to fulfill these promises (Habakkuk 2:3). However, He had not revealed that time to anyone, not even to His own prophets (1 Peter 1:10–12). Waiting for the *fullness of time* required centuries of patience because God works according to His own calendar. In fact, He measures time much differently than we do: "With the Lord one day is as a thousand years, and a thousand years as one day" (2 Peter 3:8, NASB).

When the angels announced the birth of Christ, with their tidings of peace (Luke 2:14), God declared that His promises were finally being fulfilled. The Apostle Paul interprets the *fullness of time* as the moment when God's people could at last claim their promised inheritance.[2]

In other words, God fulfilled His promises at just the right moment. The world was ready, and at the *fullness of time*, God sent His son. Many years ago I heard the prince of preachers, Dr. Adrian Rogers, share a powerful sermon and I remember him saying : "With God, time means nothing, but timing is everything."

That was true on the first Christmas, and it is still true today. I'll repeat it as a reminder: God is never early. He is never late. He always arrives in our lives at just the right time.

This is true of His presence but is also true of His provision. Some of you may be struggling this Christmas to make ends meet. We have all experienced times when it feels like there is more month than money. But get this: God is the master of *just-in-time inventorying*. That means that He doesn't always like to let resources just sit on the shelf. Instead, He stocks the storehouse of lives at the right time or just in-the-nick-of-time. Or, as Paul says, in the *fullness of time*.

And while His coming and even His provision may surprise us, it's never unplanned and unintentional by our sovereign God.

LOOK WHO'S HERE

Vance Havner, the popular country preacher from generations ago, preached a sermon entitled *Look Who's Here*. He set up the message by referring to the response we all have when a surprise guest drops by our house: "Look who's here!" He then preached through the Bible, highlighting times when Jesus showed up unexpectedly and changed everything. Havner said:

"Don't you think Moses, after a discouraging day, may have pulled open his tent flap to see the pillar of fire high in the sky and said, 'Everything's fine, *look who's here*.'

And what about Daniel, a charter member of the Lion's Club. He laid his head on the mane of a lion and said, 'I'm not afraid. *Look who's here*.'

King Nebuchadnezzar had those three fellas thrown in the fire, but when he looked down he saw four. Shadrach and company were just fine. *Look who's here.*

And what about Elijah? Water was scarce, and still, he ordered twelve barrels to be poured upon the altar. God or Baal? Choose you this day whom ye will serve! Ol' Elijah just chuckled to himself and said, '*Look who's here*.'

David, the shepherd boy who would become King, looked at Goliath, loaded his slingshot, and said, 'Your time's up. *Look who's here*.'

Jesus was born in a manger cradle surrounded by animals and angels. The angels would tell the shepherds, '*Look who's here*.'

Lazarus had been dead four days when Jesus said, 'Roll the stone away.' But Lazarus walked out of that tomb because Almighty God turned death on its heels and said, '*Look who's here*.'

One of these days—it may be at morn when the day is awakened, it may be at midday, it may be at twilight, it may be perchance in the blackness of midnight—in one mighty shout around the world we will look up and cry 'Hallelujah! He's back! *Look who's here!*'"[3]

My prayer for you is that Christmas would come to your heart and home this year like never before. And remember that when Jesus comes to us, He often comes unexpectedly—just like that first Christmas. We can be minding our own business, sitting in a field watching sheep, and out of nowhere, He shows up. *Look who's here!*

For me, the night I first met Jesus was exactly like that. I had no thought of giving my life to Him. Instead, I was minding my own business and doing my own thing when He showed up. Through the testimony of a friend from high school, Jesus arrived and changed the entire trajectory of my life.

Indeed, Christmas comes unexpectedly in our world and in our lives—just like someone showing up on Christmas day wrapped in a box. Jesus showed up that first Christmas "wrapped in cloths and lying in a manger" (Luke 2:12, NIV). This Christmas, as you see the boxes wrapped under the tree, allow them to remind you of the greatest gift of all. Take time to reflect on Jesus wrapped in His cloths, entering the world unexpectedly, to show up just for you! Allow yourself to really *look who's here*, and invite Him more deeply into the reality of your Christmas.

REFLECTION QUESTIONS

1. Can you remember a Christmas surprise that has impacted your life? Consider how Jesus can show up unexpectedly and do the same thing.

2. When was the last time that you experienced a waiting season? Can you reflect back to that time and see now how God was working through it?

3. What tough area of your life do you need to shift your perspective so that you can look up and say, "Look who's here!"? Find comfort in knowing that Jesus is with you through all of the good and the bad.

CHAPTER 2

CHRISTMAS COMES IN THE MIDDLE OF CHAOS

While Christmas comes unexpectedly, it also comes in times of difficulty and chaos. Connie Owen of South Milwaukee, Wisconsin, found that to be abundantly true. Here's what she wrote:

"In June 2003, I buried my 26-year-old son. The following Christmas was the worst of my life. I was consumed with grief to my very core. As I awoke early Christmas morning, I decided to write a few Christmas cards, belated or not. I went to the drawer where I stored the boxed cards. The drawer would only open slightly; something was jamming it. The cause of the jam was an unlabeled cassette. I had no idea what was on it or how it had gotten there. I popped the cassette in the player and waited to hear whatever mystery it held. Soon I heard my own voice. In a whisper, I say, 'It's Christmas morning, and Kyle is still sleeping.' Kyle awakens and sleepily comes to the realization that he gets to check the tree. His childish voice goes on to name his toys from Santa. The last words on the tape are both heartfelt and heartbreaking. They are three-year-old Kyle saying, 'Merry Christmas, Mom!' I know my son made this Christmas miracle happen, so I could have a smile in my heart that morning."[1]

Let's face it, Christmas can be a very difficult time of the year. In fact, it often comes in the middle of chaos. Such was the case with the first Christmas and the years immediately following Jesus' arrival. Some scholars believe that the year Jesus was born was a very violent one. Here's what Philip Jenkins has to say in his Biblical commentary about the historical context that Jesus was born into:

"Scholars differ on the exact birth date of Jesus of Nazareth, though a fair consensus holds that it was not in the year 1.

Many favor a date in or around 4 BC, and for the sake of

argument let us take that as accurate. If so, the birth occurred during or near a truly dreadful time in the history of what was already a troubled and turbulent land.

By 4 BC, Herod the Great was coming to the end of a long career that was bloody and paranoid even by the standards of Hellenistic monarchies. He ruled through tactics of mass terror and widespread surveillance that sometimes sound like a foretaste of the Stalin years.

Herod had killed multiple members of his family, and in the year 4 BC was in the process of trying and executing his son Antipater for alleged treason. He also systematically wiped out all male claimants from the old Hasmonean royal dynasty. No matter how violent, palace intrigues need not have a wider public impact, but Herod's growing paranoia and mental illness was becoming a scandal among other rulers and was presumably well known to any educated member of the Jewish elite."[2]

Talk about chaos! After a visit from the wise men who informed him of the Messiah's birth, Herod plotted multiple wicked plans to murder Him. He hoped to eliminate another perceived threat to his throne and paranoid ego.

This is the kind of world that the Savior of the Universe was born into; one of political chaos, paranoid politicians, wars, conflicts, religious nationalism, and Roman oppression. You have to wonder how Jesus' parents must have felt about the task of keeping the Christ safe.

Herod not only tried to kill Jesus directly, but he also tried to kill Him indirectly. He gave an executive order that all boys under the age of two within the vicinity of Bethlehem must be killed. He planned to sweep Jesus up in his deadly net. However, being a protective Father, God had other plans. He spoke to both the wise men and Joseph to ensure Jesus' safety, which didn't make Herod a very happy man:

> *And having been warned in a dream not to go back to Herod, they returned to their country by another route.*
>
> *When they had gone, an angel of the Lord appeared to Joseph in a dream. "Get up," he said, "take the child and his mother and escape to Egypt. Stay there until I tell you, for Herod is going to search for the child to kill Him..."*
>
> *...When Herod realized that he had been outwitted by the Magi, he was furious, and he gave orders to kill all the boys in Bethlehem and its vicinity who were two years old and under, in accordance with the time he had learned from the Magi.* (Matthew 2:12-16, NIV)

Christmas comes. The first Christmas came in the middle of intense chaos. And today, Christmas may find you dealing with your own chaotic issues.

They say 'tis the season, correct?

"Deck the halls with boughs of holly
Fa la la la la, la la la la.
'Tis the season to be jolly
Fa la la la la, la la la la.
Don we now our gay apparel
Fa la la la la, la la la la.
Troll the ancient Yuletide carol
Fa la la la la, la la la la."[3]

Jolly is the way we're supposed to feel around Christmas time, right? And for many of us, it is. Hopefully, Christmas is a season of great joy, and you can't wait for it to come each year.

But some of you reading this can't wait for Christmas to leave. I'm not talking about the birth of Jesus, Christmas. But the other side of Christmas. The one that puts pressure on your emotions, relationships, finances, and time. That can cause negative emotions to rise to the surface, fill you with more sadness than joy, and make your life more chaotic than calm.

Strangely, a season known for its *jolliness* can also be a time of sadness or even depression. Yet, you still walk from store to store and go from party to party; meanwhile, your heart grows heavier and heavier. From my experience, there are two main *joy thieves* that want to steal your joy this Christmas.

JOY THIEVES

#1 The Joy Thief of Grief

Perhaps your heart is sad this season because you are grieving the loss of a loved one. As a pastor for over thirty years, I know first-hand how difficult emotions can be around Christmas. Whether it's the first Christmas without a loved one or the fiftieth one, it's always difficult. When there's so much focus on family, it can be extremely challenging for those of us who are missing family.

If grief is your source of Christmastime depression, let me encourage you: the first Christmas gives hope to every subsequent Christmas. Jesus' arrival, death, and resurrection means there is hope for those who grieve and weep over the loss of loved ones at Christmas.

The Apostle Paul gave some especially good encouragement for people who are missing loved ones at Christmas:

> *Brothers and sisters, we do not want you to be uninformed about those who sleep in death, so that you do not grieve like the rest of*

mankind, who have no hope. For we believe that Jesus died and rose again, and so we believe that God will bring with Jesus those who have fallen asleep in him. According to the Lord's word, we tell you that we who are still alive, who are left until the coming of the Lord, will certainly not precede those who have fallen asleep. For the Lord himself will come down from heaven, with a loud command, with the voice of the archangel and with the trumpet call of God, and the dead in Christ will rise first. After that, we who are still alive and are left will be caught up together with them in the clouds to meet the Lord in the air. And so we will be with the Lord forever. Therefore encourage one another with these words. (1 Thessalonians 4:13-18, NIV)

Did you catch that? We do not grieve as those who have no hope. Indeed, there is a difference between how a believer and non-Christian approach grief. A non-Christian weeps through the tear pools of a hopeless heart. We, however, weep with the hope that we will see our loved ones again! The following story perfectly illustrates the difference between grieving as a Christian and as a non-believer:

"Dr. George W. Truett, a longtime pastor, told a story about a funeral he once conducted for a beautiful little six-year-old girl who had tragically died. Her mother was a devoted member of his church, but her father was not a Christian. During the funeral, Dr. Truett did the best he could to offer comfort and hope to family and friends who were mourning. When he finished the message, he walked down and stood beside the open casket. People came one-by-one and looked at the beautiful little girl lying there in that silk-lined casket. Finally, the daddy came. The great big, hulking he-man approached humbly and slowly. He reached the casket, held onto the edge of it as his hands trembled. Tears streamed down his cheeks as he looked at the cold, lifeless form of his precious baby girl. He looked at her and said, 'Oh. My baby, you are gone. You are gone. Gone. Goodbye forever.' Then, heartbreakingly, he turned and walked away.

Afterward, Dr. Truett observed the girl's sweet little mother come to the casket. She stood there, reached over, and with her finger, she twirled one of those little blonde curls. She straightened the ruffle of the little girl's dress and then leaned over to kiss her cold cheek.

The mother said, 'My darling, you've only been with us for six years, but these have been six wonderful, joyous years. And now my precious little one, I say to you, *Goodnight*, because Mama will see you and the Lord in the morning.'"⁴

One came to the casket and said, "Goodbye." The other went to the casket and said, "Goodnight." That's the difference that Christmas can make; the difference that the coming of Christ into our hearts can make. Because Jesus came, we have the hope that we will see our loved ones who have died again. Remember those Christmas presents under your tree? Jesus wrapped Himself in human flesh for us. As painful as this season may be, thank God for the hope that He gives us to see our loved ones again. The best way to fight back against the joy thief of grief is through the triumph of gratitude.

THE BEST WAY TO FIGHT BACK AGAINST THE JOY THIEF OF GRIEF IS THROUGH THE TRIUMPH OF GRATITUDE.

#2 The Joy Thief of Anger

We all have our favorite Christmas traditions that get us in the mood for the holidays. One of our family's traditions is watching the movie *Elf*. In the movie, Will Farrell plays the part of Buddy the Elf, and in one of my favorite scenes, he encounters a little person at his father's office. In the back and forth exchange between Buddy and the little person—who Buddy mistakes as an elf from Santa's workshop—Buddy calls him an "angry elf."

Unfortunately, during the Christmas season, you can encounter many angry elves out there. You may see them on the streets leading to the shopping centers, at the mall on Black Friday, or at the office Christmas party. You may even be tempted to become an angry elf yourself.

Don't get me wrong, we should never aim to be angry elves, but not all anger is necessarily bad. There is such a thing as "holy anger." We see a picture of holy anger in the Old Testament book of Nehemiah:

Now, the men and their wives raised a great outcry against their fellow Jews. Some were saying, "We and our sons and daughters are numerous; in order for us to eat and stay alive, we must get grain."

Others were saying, "We are mortgaging our fields, our vineyards and our homes to get grain during the famine."

Still others were saying, "We have had to borrow money to pay the king's tax on our fields and vineyards. Although we are of the same flesh and blood as our fellow Jews and though our children are as good as theirs, yet we have to subject our sons and daughters to slavery. Some of our daughters have already been enslaved, but we are powerless, because our fields and our vineyards belong to others."

When I heard their outcry and these charges, I was very angry.
(Nehemiah 5:1-6, NIV)

Nehemiah—the man who helped God's people rebuild Jerusalem—had righteous and holy anger against the injustices among his society.

Some things should make us righteously angry this Christmas. We should be angry about the treatment of immigrants, the marginalized, the homeless, and the fatherless. Indeed, there are social justice causes that should ignite a passion in our lives and lead to positive action. This is what we call holy anger.

Unfortunately, for many people, Christmas will not be marked by *holy anger* but by *hellish anger*. You might be tempted to get quick with your spouse, honk your horn on the freeway, or push to get to the front of the line at stores. This type of anger is produced by stress and steals our joy right out from underneath us.

Have you ever heard about Rudolph's Rage Room? CBS News first reported on it back in 2017. According to the report, the pressure of preparing for Christmas was pushing some Londoners over the edge. While many were getting into the holiday spirit, others were escaping underground to relieve some stress.

Rudolph's Rage Room provided a place where people could take out all of their frustrations. For the price of twenty-five dollars, they were given a baseball bat and three minutes to smash everything inside of the rage room.

One Londoner said, "By this date, I think people are pretty sick of the Christmas music—all the decorations—I think people are done with it and wanna get out some of that stress."

Another commented, "I just imagined everyone from last Christmas who didn't get me anything and then showed them how it was."[5]

Obviously, Christmas can sometimes bring out the worst in us.

Each of us needs to take extra precaution not to let our anger get the best of us during the Christmas season. If you aren't careful, your emotions might rob you of the joy that God wants you to experience this Christmas.

In his book *How To Deal With How You Feel*, Ralph Spees says, "Bitterness damages relationships, deteriorates our personality, and defiles and destroys our spiritual vitality. Unfortunately, over time, this very thing that we might think only is a part of the unredeemed heart can happen to us Christians as well."[6]

Take the advice of the author of Hebrews: "Make every effort to live in peace with everyone and to be holy; without holiness no one will see the Lord. See to it that no one falls short of the grace of God and that no bitter root grows up to cause trouble and defile many" (Hebrews 12:14-15, NIV). Without a doubt, Christmas comes in the middle of chaos. Navigating that chaos in an honorable and holy way takes intentional effort on our end.

IMMANUEL

Let's look back at the first Christmas for some further reference. Before Herod attempted to kill Jesus, the Bible gives insight into his underlying anger and the implications it had on an entire country:

After Jesus was born in Bethlehem in Judea, during the time of King Herod, Magi from the east came to Jerusalem and asked, "Where is the one who has been born king of the Jews? We saw his star when it rose and have come to worship him."

When King Herod heard this he was disturbed, and all Jerusalem with him. (Matthew 2:1-3, NIV)

That last verse may contain one of the most downplayed statements in the entire Bible: "Herod was disturbed and all Jerusalem with him." If the volatile and paranoid Herod was disturbed, upset, and angry, then the entire nation would undoubtedly be on pins and needles.

Herod was appointed by the Roman Empire to be the king but he was actually a foreigner, and was not from Israel. He was a cruel and vicious ruler who didn't care about the Israelites. When Herod came to power, he inherited a Jewish governing body called the Sanhedrin. The Sanhedrin was like the Supreme Court of that day and was made up of seventy-one men. But when Herod stepped in as king, he had forty-five Sanhedrin members killed because they didn't blindly follow his every brash order. So when the Bible says that "Herod was disturbed and all Jerusalem with him," trust me, they were deeply disturbed.

Such was the chaotic world into which Jesus was born. And such may be the world in which Christmas comes to you this year. That chaos might be brought on by intense grief, seething anger, financial stress, or unrealistic expectations. Regardless of the source, I believe we can overcome it through the power of the One who came that first Christmas. Let these verses serve as your strength this holiday:

I can do everything through Christ, who gives me strength.
(Philippians 4:13, NLT)

...greater is he that is in you, than he that is in the world. (1 John 4:4, KJV)

No, in all these things we are more than conquerors through him who loved us. (Romans 8:37, NIV)

What I'm trying to say is that no matter how chaotic your circumstances, or how dark your nights may be, there is hope in the Christ of Christmas. He specializes in bringing hope into dark and difficult places.

Alexander Maclaren, the great Scottish preacher, once told a story about himself that reminds us of how God enters into the chaos and darkness of our lives.

When he was sixteen years old, he got his first job in the city of Glasgow. He lived with his family on a farm about six or eight miles from the city. He would work in the city all week long, stay there, and then walk home on the weekends to be with his family. Between the farmhouse where his family lived and the city of Glasgow was a very deep, dark, and dangerous ravine. Many people had been attacked, mugged, robbed, and even killed there. Understandably so, Alexander was deathly afraid of that dark ravine.

On the first Monday morning of Alex's job his daddy walked him into the city. When they arrived, his father looked at him and said: "Alex, son, when you get off work on Friday afternoon, I want you to come home immediately because it is going to be a long week for me and your mother. We're not used to being apart from you, so come on home Friday."

Alexander Maclaren thought about that deep, dark valley and how he would have to walk through it on that Friday night. He said, "Well, Dad, I'm going to be really tired from working all week long. What I'd like to do is just stay in the city Friday night and walk on home on Saturday morning."

His dad said, "No, son, no, we're going to miss you too much. I want you to come home Friday night."

Alexander Maclaren worked all week long in fear and dread of walking through that dark valley on Friday night. There wasn't a day that passed that he wasn't anxious and afraid.

Finally, Friday came and he packed his belongings, got out on the road, and began to walk down the dark road. As he walked, he whistled to keep his courage up. He talked out loud to an imaginary companion along the way. Finally, he came to the edge of that dark ravine. Tears welled up in his eyes. He just couldn't bring himself to walk down into that dark, dark valley alone. As he stood there, he heard something—something was stirring down in that ravine. He was paralyzed with fear. He couldn't run; he couldn't do anything.

Suddenly, up out of that ravine came the face and figure of the man he loved most on the earth. It was his daddy. His father said, "Alex, I missed you so much and I came out here to meet you to walk home with you."

Alexander Maclaren said that on that night, shoulder to shoulder and side by side, he and his father walked down into that dark, dark valley and out the other side. He was not afraid because his father was with him.[7]

I don't know what dark ravine or valley you may be walking through this Christmas, but I do know that God has said, "I'll never leave you nor forsake you" (Hebrews 13:5, ESV). When you think about it, this is the meaning of Christmas—Jesus is always there.

One of the great Christmas catchwords is *Immanuel*. Here's what the Bible has to say about that word in the Christmas story:

> *"The virgin will conceive and give birth to a son, and they will call him Immanuel" (which means "God with us")*. (Matthew 1:23, NIV)

God is with us. Take a moment and say this under your breath: "God is with me." Repeat it: "God is with me." Say it louder now: "God is with me." That's good news, isn't it?

No matter where you go, God is with you. He is with you in the darkness, through the valleys, and even during the depths of difficulty. David knew this and wrote:

> *Even though I walk through the darkest valley, I will fear no evil, for you are with me; your rod and your staff, they comfort me.*
> (Psalms 23:4, NIV)

Paul knew this to be true, as well:

Who shall separate us from the love of Christ? Shall trouble or hardship or persecution or famine or nakedness or danger or sword?

As it is written: "For your sake we face death all day long; we are considered as sheep to be slaughtered."

No, in all these things we are more than conquerors through him who loved us. For I am convinced that neither death nor life, neither angels nor demons, neither the present nor the future, nor any powers, neither height nor depth, nor anything else in all creation, will be able to separate us from the love of God that is in Christ Jesus our Lord." (Romans 8:35-39, NIV)

Immanuel—God is with you! He is with you in the good times and in the bad times. In times of chaos and challenge. Just like on that first Christmas, it's true today that Christmas comes in the middle of difficulty! And because of that, there is hope in the chaos.

REFLECTION QUESTIONS

1. What chaos in your life is trying to distract you from the true meaning of Christmas this year?

2. Have the thieves of grief or anger been stealing away your Christmas joy? What are some tangible ways that you can express gratitude and live an intentional life of peace to combat these negative influences?

3. Are you facing a dark ravine of fear, worry, discouragement, or depression this Christmas? How can you apply the truth of God's Word to your situation and remind yourself that Immanuel is always with you no matter what?

CHAPTER 3

CHRISTMAS COMES BECAUSE WE NEED IT

I remember it like it was yesterday. It was December of 1986, and I was one of many students seated in Raley Chapel at Oklahoma Baptist University for our last service before Christmas break. Now for those who have attended chapel weekly at a Christian University, you know that it's not always riveting and life-changing. Often, you go to the services because it's a graduation requirement. Very seldom do students hear something so impactful that they'd write about it thirty-five years later—like I'm doing now! But this chapel service was different for me. It was so life-altering that I actually recounted it when I was asked to speak at a chapel service for my alma-mater twenty years after graduation.

Pastors or professors would usually be the ones to preach at chapel. But at this service, a student was asked to share the events that unfolded in his life the previous Christmas. It ended up being a heart-wrenching story.

He had been preparing for fall semester finals when he received a call from his father, who lived overseas. It was the type of call that you hope to never get. The student's father informed him that his younger brother—his only brother—was sick and in the hospital. His dad explained that they thought it was best to fly home and be with the family. So, the older brother did exactly that, thinking he would return in time for finals week. However, when his plane landed, he was met by his dad with devastating news: during the flight, his little brother had passed away.

As you can imagine, the dad and his oldest son exchanged many tears and a long embrace. Because it was so close to Christmas, the older brother's parents convinced him to stay at home for the holidays. Due to the circumstances, he made arrangements with his professors to make up his final exams upon returning the first of the year.

The following week, the family hosted a funeral and said their goodbyes and then prepared to celebrate Christmas. As he told the story, the young student indicated that despite the grief of losing his brother, their family had an enjoyable Christmas together. They took part in all of their traditional Christmas activities: cooking turkey, spending precious family time together, and celebrating the birth of Jesus Christ.

On Christmas morning, the family tradition was for the oldest child, who was now the only child, to pass out the gifts from underneath the tree. Gifts were handed out, unwrapped, and enjoyed. Through all of the grief, there was an infusion of joy that morning. This family came to understand that Christmas really does come in the middle of chaos.

After all the gifts were opened, there was still one more Christmas surprise. Stuck way behind the tree, where nobody could see until all of the presents were gone, was one small, poorly wrapped gift. After further examination, the older brother discovered that it was addressed to "Dad" in the writing of his recently deceased little brother. Apparently, the younger son had purchased a gift, wrapped it himself, and hid it under the tree just days before being hospitalized. As one might imagine, the older son carried that little gift with great care to his dad, who was seated in his reclining chair. The father began trembling as his hands unwrapped the paper and unwrapped a special memory from his recently deceased son. When he finally tore the paper off, the dad saw through tear-filled eyes that the package contained a cheap, gaudy, plastic pencil holder. It wasn't a gift that one would generally cherish. However, the words on the bottom of this pencil holder made it perhaps the most important gift this dad would ever receive. It simply read: "Dad, I Love You."

One of the greatest lessons of Christmas and life is this: The greatest gifts are gifts of love. There's never been a better demonstration of a love-filled gift than Jesus Christ. His arrival on earth that first Christmas set the stage for his sinless life and, ultimately, his sacrificial death. In the same way that the youngest brother's pencil sharpener showed deep love to his father, Jesus' death on a cross shows His deep love for us. The sharpener was cheap, gaudy, and plastic—just like the cross was rugged, wooden, and blood-stained. But the message God inscribed on it was, "I Love You!"

Christmas comes for many different reasons, but perhaps the most important is because we desperately need it. God knew that we needed Christmas because He knew that we needed Jesus. Our Savior lived a sinless life and then died the death on the cross that we deserved so that our sins could be forgiven. You see, we need the message of Christmas first and foremost because we are sinners in need of God's mercy.

Perhaps, the saddest Christmas verse in the entire Bible is found in the story of Jesus' birth:

Then she gave birth to her firstborn Son, and she wrapped Him snugly in cloth and laid Him in a feeding trough—because there was no room for them at the lodging place. (Luke 2:7, HCSB)

At Jesus' birth, there was no room for Him anywhere! No room for the Son of God. No room for the Savior of the world. No room for the Prince of Peace. Yet, Jesus chose to be born into uncomfortable and unlikely circumstances anyways. Not because He needs us, but because we desperately need Him.

However, maybe the sweetest verse in all the Bible explains the significance of His birth:

For God loved the world in this way: He gave His One and Only Son, so that everyone who believes in Him will not perish but have eternal life. (John 3:16, HCSB)

Did you get that? God loved the world. God loves you. God loves your family. God loves your neighbors. God loves everyone.

It makes me think of a familiar scene from popular love movies throughout history. It goes something like this: When people were love struck for the first time, they'd pick a flower and pull off the petals one by one. As each petal fell to the ground, they'd say, "She loves me, she loves me not. She loves me, she loves me not." It's symbolic of the way we try to find security in the love of other humans, even though it's imperfect and fleeting. It's not like that with God! At the dropping of every petal you can say, "He loves me! He loves me! He loves me! He loves me!"

However, one major issue affects God's ability to share His love fully with us. That issue is our sin. Our sin separates us from the holy presence of God. And that is why Jesus came that first Christmas, to redeem us sinners back to God.

God loves us. Sin separates us. Jesus came to redeem us.

Separation from God isn't because His love is absent but rather because our sin is present. Thankfully, God's love is bigger than our sin. Because of that love, He created an opportunity for imperfect people to have a relationship with a perfect God.

Let's pick the story up from the very beginning.

WE ALL HAVE SINNED

This story starts all the way back at the creation of the world in the Garden of Eden. You probably know the account of Adam and Eve, the first humans to ever roam the planet. God placed them in the Garden, which was like Heaven on Earth, and gave them all kinds of freedom. However, there was one stipulation:

> And the Lord God commanded the man, "You are free to eat from any tree of the garden, but you must not eat from the tree of the knowledge of good and evil, for on the day you eat from it, you will certainly die." (Genesis 2:16-17, HCSB)

Talk about temptation! Our human nature always wants us to do the one thing that's off-limits. It reminds me of the time Mark Twain once humorously quipped, "I can resist everything but temptation."

That was true for Adam and Eve, it is true for us today, and it has been true for everyone who has ever lived. As the story goes on, here's what the Bible tells us:

Now the serpent was the most cunning of all the wild animals that the Lord God had made. He said to the woman, "Did God really say, 'You can't eat from any tree in the garden'?"

The woman said to the serpent, "We may eat the fruit from the trees in the garden. But about the fruit of the tree in the middle of the garden, God said, 'You must not eat it or touch it, or you will die.'"

"No! You will not die," the serpent said to the woman. "In fact, God knows that when you eat it your eyes will be opened and you will be like God, knowing good and evil." Then the woman saw that the tree was good for food and delightful to look at, and that it was desirable for obtaining wisdom. So she took some of its fruit and ate it; she also gave some to her husband, who was with her, and he ate it. Then the eyes of both of them were opened, and they knew they were naked; so they sewed fig leaves together and made loincloths for themselves. (Genesis 3:1-7, HCSB)

Just like that, we are introduced to a concept called *original sin*. The Apostle Paul would elaborate on this in the book of Romans:

Therefore, just as sin entered the world through one man, and death through sin, in this way death spread to all men, because all sinned. (Romans 5:12, HCSB)

Everyone has sinned. And that sin naturally separates us from God. In 1886, Scottish author Robert Louis Stevenson wrote a novella that reflected a disturbing truth about humanity titled *The Strange Case of Dr. Jekyll and Mr. Hyde.* It's a story of a respected physician and medical researcher who embodied the very best Victorian ideals of morality and decency. However, experiments on himself revealed the murderous savage within him that had been lurking in the shadows of his gentle public demeanor.[1] The famous saying, *Jekyll and Hyde,* originates from the character in this novella. It speaks to our dual nature—one that is outwardly good, but sometimes inwardly dark.

The point is that all of us have a sin nature. Even when it's not on full display, it's always lurking in the shadows. Behind every Dr. Jekyll is a Mr. Hyde. As Mark Twain said, "Everyone is a moon and has a dark side which he never shows anybody."[2]

In the book of Romans, the Apostle Paul goes to great lengths to explain the universal problem of human depravity. It's what we might call the *dark side of the moon.*

> *What then? Are we any better? Not at all! For we have previously charged that both Jews and Gentiles are all under sin, as it is written:*
>
>> *There is no one righteous, not even one.*
>> *There is no one who understands;*
>> *there is no one who seeks God.*
>> *All have turned away;*
>> *all alike have become useless.*
>> *There is no one who does what is good,*
>> *not even one.*
>> *Their throat is an open grave;*
>> *they deceive with their tongues.*
>> *Vipers' venom is under their lips.*
>> *Their mouth is full of cursing and bitterness.*
>> *Their feet are swift to shed blood;*
>> *ruin and wretchedness are in their paths,*

and the path of peace they have not known.
There is no fear of God before their eyes. (Romans 3:9-18, HCSB)

Let's break the Scripture down a little further. In verse ten, Paul says, "There is no one righteous, not even one." What does that mean? Simple—it means exactly what it says. None of us are without sin. It was true in Paul's day, and it's still true in our day. Honestly, *the dark side of the moon* gets even darker as you read the Bible. The reality is that the very best we have to offer is still sin. In the Old Testament, the prophet Isaiah backs up verse ten of Romans chapter three when he puts it this way: "All of us have become like something unclean, and all our righteous acts are like a polluted garment; all of us wither like a leaf, and our iniquities carry us away like the wind" (Isaiah 64:6, HCSB).

As Paul continues writing, in verse eleven, he says, "There is no one who understands; there is no one who seeks God." Wow! Not only are we sinners by nature, but by nature, we also don't seek God on our own. That gets us to the heart of Christmas. When we weren't searching for God, God came searching for us. You see, Christmas was never our idea. We didn't dial the phone number of Heaven and ask God to send His son because we were in desperate need of a Savior! No way—in our state of depravity, we weren't even able to recognize that we needed saving. Christmas was God's idea from the very beginning. He thought of us long before we ever thought of Him.

WHEN WE WEREN'T SEARCHING FOR GOD, GOD CAME SEARCHING FOR US.

Frances Thompson captured this idea in his poem, *The Hound of Heaven*:

"I FLED Him, down the nights and down the days;
I fled Him, down the arches of the years;
I fled Him, down the labyrinthine ways
Of my own mind; and in the mist of tears
I hid from Him, and under running laughter.
Up vistaed hopes I sped;
And shot, precipitated,
Adown Titanic glooms of chasmèd fears,
From those strong Feet that followed, followed after.
But with unhurrying chase,
And unperturbèd pace,
Deliberate speed, majestic instancy,
They beat—and a Voice beat
More instant than the Feet—
'All things betray thee, who betrayest Me.'" [3]

That poem perfectly captures the severity of our sin problem. In our sin, we had no desire to seek God, choosing instead to flee from Him. Therefore, it is God who had to chase us down. And when He caught up to us, because of our sin, what we really deserved was judgment.

WE ALL DESERVE JUDGEMENT FOR OUR SIN

As I stated earlier, sin separates us from God. And if left unchecked, it will separate us from God for all eternity. Make no mistake, sin carries a high price tag both in your present life and in the afterlife. As many old-time preachers used to say: "Sin will take you further than you want to go, keep you longer than you want to stay, and cost you more than you want to pay."

Certainly, that was the case with Adam and Eve:

Then the man and his wife heard the sound of the Lord God walking in the garden at the time of the evening breeze, and they hid themselves from the Lord God among the trees of the garden. So the Lord God called out to the man and said to him, "Where are you?"

And he said, "I heard You in the garden and I was afraid because I was naked, so I hid."

Then He asked, "Who told you that you were naked? Did you eat from the tree that I commanded you not to eat from?"

Then the man replied, "The woman You gave to be with me—she gave me some fruit from the tree, and I ate."

So the Lord God asked the woman, "What is this you have done?"

And the woman said, "It was the serpent. He deceived me, and I ate."

Then the Lord God said to the serpent:

> *"Because you have done this,*
> *you are cursed more than any livestock*
> *and more than any wild animal.*
> *You will move on your belly*
> *and eat dust all the days of your life.*
> *I will put hostility between you and the woman,*
> *and between your seed and her seed.*
> *He will strike your head,*
> *and you will strike his heel.*

He said to the woman:
I will intensify your labor pains;
you will bear children in anguish.
Your desire will be for your husband,
yet he will rule over you."

And He said to Adam, *"Because you listened to your wife's voice
and ate from the tree about which I commanded you, 'Don't eat
from it':*

The ground is cursed because of you.
You will eat from it by means of painful labor
all the days of your life.
It will produce thorns and thistles for you,
and you will eat the plants of the field.
You will eat bread by the sweat of your brow
until you return to the ground,
since you were taken from it.
For you are dust,
and you will return to dust." (Genesis 3:8-19, HCSB)

As you can see, sin resulted in a high cost for Adam and Eve. God's intention for them was a life of Heaven on Earth, but they ended up with a life that was cursed because of their sin. Furthermore, their sin resulted in a high cost for the rest of humanity throughout history. Paul puts it this way: "Therefore, just as sin entered the world through one man, and death through sin, in this way death spread to all men, because all sinned" (Romans 5:12, HCSB).

Sin results in death. And not just physical death, but something the Bible calls eternal death. John, who was granted a vision of the end times, wrote in the book of Revelation: "Death and Hades were thrown into the lake of fire. This is the second death, the lake of fire" (Revelation 20:14, HCSB). Simply put—death, the result of sin, is a punishment that lasts forever and ever.

Oh, but how the coming of Christ changes all of this! He provided a new possibility for life. The first Christmas not only brought hope to the world but hope for your life as well. The birth of Jesus was the ultimate second chance.

How many of you love a second chance? Just say amen, right there where you are reading, if you do. As a golfer, I'm all about second chances. The official golf word for it is a *mulligan*. If you play with a benevolent golfing partner, they might give you a mulligan whenever you hit a ball into the water or the woods. A second chance. A do-over. Free of charge.

That is exactly what the coming of Christ on that first Christmas signaled to the world. It let us know that we have a benevolent Heavenly Father who loves us enough to give us a second chance. As a matter of fact, almost every verse on judgment is connected to a spiritual mulligan. Check it out:

> *For the wages of sin is death, but the gift of God is eternal life in Christ Jesus our Lord.* (Romans 6:23, HCSB)

> *...so that, just as sin reigned in death, so also grace will reign through righteousness, resulting in eternal life through Jesus Christ our Lord.* (Romans 5:21, HCSB)

That's why the books in the Bible about Jesus' life are called *The Gospels*, or *Good News*. Because while it is true that we all have sinned, and we all deserve judgment for our sin, it is equally true that we all can be forgiven of our sin!

WE ALL CAN BE FORGIVEN FROM OUR SIN

I, for one, am so thankful for the forgiveness of sin that was made possible because of the coming of Jesus on that first Christmas.

For centuries now, those that are followers of Christ have called this grace. There's an acronym that paints a wonderful picture of what grace is:

God's
Riches
At
Christ's
Expense

That's grace! And it is for anyone willing to ask God to forgive them of their sin. No wonder one of the most popular songs in the 2,000-year history of the church is *Amazing Grace*. It was written by John Newton, who was a former slave ship master—a profession in which he worked for several years. Over and over again, he would bring slaves from Africa to England by boat. He's on record admitting to sometimes treating the slaves abhorrently. In 1754, after becoming violently ill on a sea voyage, Newton abandoned his life as a slave trader and wholeheartedly devoted his life to God.

Twelve years later, he was ordained as an Anglican priest, becoming quite popular as a preacher and hymn writer. In fact, he penned some 280 hymns, the greatest among them being *Amazing Grace*:

"Amazing Grace, how sweet the sound
That saved a wretch like me
I once was lost, but now am found
Was blind but now I see

Was Grace that taught my heart to fear
And Grace, my fears relieved
How precious did that Grace appear
The hour I first believed

Through many dangers, toils and snares
We have already come
T'was grace that brought us safe thus far
And Grace will lead us home
And Grace will lead us home

Amazing Grace, how sweet the sound
That saved a wretch like me
I once was lost but now am found
Was blind but now I see
Was blind, but now I see"[4]

Understanding the story behind that hymn adds so much depth to our understanding of God's grace. John Newton knew the terrible sins that he had committed against other humans. He also knew that those sins deserved death. But instead of meeting John with punishment, God pursued John with the invitation of grace. It was at Christ's expense; Jesus died so that John could experience the undeserved freedom of forgiveness.

Christmas comes and brings with it the message of grace, peace, and hope. But why did Christmas come? Because we desperately need it. And God understood this need before we ever did. John talks about it in his Gospel:

For God did not send His Son into the world that He might condemn the world, but that the world might be saved through Him. (John 3:17, HCSB)

Jesus came because we needed Him. He came because He loved us. And remember, the greatest gifts in life are always gifts of love.

I remember the first Christmas I came to understand this truth as a young child. I was in fourth grade, and like most fourth-graders,

I was excitedly looking forward to Christmas morning and all the gifts I would receive. When Christmas arrived, my parents told me that my gift was outside. *Wow,* I thought, *a gift too large to bring in the house!* I was stoked. I mean, this was going to be a better gift than Ralphie's Red Ryder BB-gun from the movie *A Christmas Story!*

I went outside, walked around the corner of our house, and then I saw it. It was a bicycle! What fourth-grade boy wouldn't want a new bike for Christmas? However, this wasn't just any new bike. I quickly realized that it was my old bike. My parents had painted it, put on a new seat, replaced the horn, and wrapped it as a present for me.

Truthfully, I was disappointed because it wasn't the brand-new bike I dreamed about. But I also found myself deeply appreciative because I realized my parents had done all they could with the resources they had. It was all to make Christmas memorable for me. Their gift represented a labor of love that taught me a valuable life lesson. The lesson being that the motive of love is the measure of any gift. Right up to the writing of this book, I had never let them know how meaningful that gift was to me.

The greatest gifts in life are always gifts of love. It could be a cheap, gaudy, plastic pencil holder, or maybe even a refurbished bike. The most important gift of all was the old, wooden, rugged, blood-stained cross. Nothing says *I love you* like gifts of love. And there isn't a greater gift of love than the gift of life that comes as a result of that first Christmas. Christmas is the most significant labor of love the world will ever see!

REFLECTION QUESTIONS

1. Where or when has God come searching for you? Examine your life and reflect upon how His love has been constantly pursuing you.

2. What sin in your life are you allowing to separate you from God? Are you willing to surrender it to Him and experience the freedom that He offers to you?

3. Do you view God as loving? If not, ask Him to help you to see Him as a caring Father.

CHAPTER 4

CHRISTMAS COMES AND
SOME REJECT IT

Christmas comes, and some reject it. Surprisingly, even some Christians think the whole idea of celebrating Christmas during the winter solstice is unspiritual and unwise. Let me explain.

Believers who advocate that it is wrong for us to celebrate Christmas often point to its connection with an ancient pagan holiday called Saturnalia. I am not an expert on this, nor do I want to be, because truthfully, I don't see any need to be! However, in ages past, pagans who worshiped the sun noticed that the days kept getting shorter and shorter in their particular hemisphere. Of course, the farther north or south you're located, the more you see that daylight is affected.

People began to notice that as December continued, the days grew shorter, and of course, the sunset happened sooner. But on December 21st, something wonderful happened. The sorry predicament of minimal daylight was reversed, and the daylight suddenly started lasting longer. It's what is now known as the winter solstice.

For these pagans, it was a cause for celebration. They thought: "The sun has come back to life, and the days aren't getting shorter! They're getting longer, once again. The darkness isn't winning anymore; the light is overpowering the darkness!"

They gave gifts to one another, and reportedly, they brought trees from outside into their houses. As part of the celebration, they decorated them and enjoyed observing their beauty during that season.

For some religious folk, this presents the issue of *guilt by association*. They think: *Here we are, Christians, treating Christmas just like the pagans! Every year, we celebrate right around the winter solstice and even decorate trees inside of our houses.*

This is why some feel celebrating Christmas is wrong. Now, I don't feel that way whatsoever, and we celebrate Christmas at my house every year. However, you won't find us worshiping the sun god; we focus entirely on Jesus. Specifically on His birth, which is what the church worldwide celebrates around this time.

Strange as it may sound to some of us, there are some legitimate Christians who reject Christmas. At least they reject the way it is celebrated in our culture today. And if this is where you fall on this issue, then more power to you. Please, don't do anything that violates your conscience.

Just as some Christians reject Christmas, unsurprisingly, more and more non-Christians reject it, just in a different way. Many aim to take Christ out of Christmas. Large corporations are opting to call it the *holiday* season instead of the *Christmas* season. They coach their employees to say, "Happy holidays" instead of "Merry Christmas" to their customers. There has even been a culture war waged over the design of a disposable cup at a certain nationwide coffee shop.

People today may vary on why they reject Christmas. Perhaps they are just not fond of the whole *Christmas cheer* aspect of the season. Maybe they are a modern-day Ebenezer Scrooge or a real-life Grinch.

As a side note, if that is you, then you might think about moving to Alaska. The self-proclaimed Christmas experts at GetCenturyLink attempted to determine which states have the most and least Christmas spirit by measuring various online behaviors. They analyzed activity like Google searches for gingerbread houses and Amazon purchases of *Elf on a Shelf* dolls. They determined that Washington and South Dakota have the most Christmas spirit, while Alaska is the Scroogeiest state of all![1] So, for all you Bah Humbugs out there, bundle up and move north as far as you can go.

Anyways, Christmas indeed comes, and some reject it. But unfortunately, their rejection often runs much deeper than not liking trees or eggnog (By the way, who actually likes eggnog?). This type of rejection runs even deeper than disdain for the commercialization of Christmas. Christmas comes, and most tragically of all, some reject because they reject Jesus Christ Himself.

Unfortunately, this is nothing new. But let me give some advice to the Christian culture warrior trying to hold non-Christians to

Christian tradition. For those demanding that everyone celebrate Christmas with coffee cups and salutations that point to Christ: stop it! There is a deeper issue at stake, and it has been going on since the very first Christmas.

Jesus' birth—the first Christmas—was not met with overwhelming acceptance and approval. Only Mary and Joseph, a few shepherds, and some wise men who were two years late for the delivery actually celebrated. It's safe to say there was not a massive fanfare surrounding the long-awaited arrival of Jesus to planet earth.

I love basketball and often think of Bible stories in terms of the NBA. Imagine what it would be like if your favorite team won the world championship on the opponent's home court, just to come home for the victory parade, and no fans showed up to celebrate. That might be the best way to visualize the way Jesus came to planet earth. It was completely anti-climatic!

Two passages in the Bible demonstrate the early and ongoing rejection of the first Christmas and Christ himself:

He came to that which was his own, but his own did not receive him. Yet to all who did receive him, to those who believed in his name, he gave the right to become children of God—children born not of natural descent, nor of human decision or a husband's will, but born of God. (John 1:11-13, NIV)

Did you catch that? John said that "He came to that which was his own, but his own did not receive him." To whom is John referring? The Jewish people—or God's very own people!

The Apostle Paul gives us a little more detail in the book of Romans:

I speak the truth in Christ—I am not lying; my conscience is testifying to me with the Holy Spirit— that I have intense sorrow and continual anguish in my heart. For I could almost wish to be cursed and cut off from the Messiah for the benefit of my brothers, my own flesh and blood. They are Israelites, and to them belong the adoption, the glory, the covenants, the giving of the law, the temple service, and the promises. The ancestors are theirs, and from them, by physical descent, came the Messiah, who is God over all, praised forever. Amen. (Romans 9:1-5, NASB)

Here Paul is lamenting the fact that his "own" did not receive him. I love that little phrase in verse five that says, "came the Messiah." It's just another reminder that Christmas Comes! It comes with force and strength, purpose and precision, power and grace. Yet, even 2,000 years ago, most Jewish people at the time of Christ's birth rejected Him.

That rejection was a huge burden on Paul's heart. There was nobody who wanted the Jews to accept Jesus as the Messiah more than Paul. He longed for his Jewish brothers and sisters to be saved. He even went so far as to say he would instantly take their place in torment to see them saved. He wrote in Romans 9:3: "For I could almost wish to be cursed and cut off from the Messiah for the benefit of my brothers, my own flesh and blood" (HCSB).

Charles Swindoll points out the irony of it all. He wrote: "Someone had already taken their place in torment. Yet they rejected the Messiah. And if they rejected the Son of God, why would they accept the same gift from a little evangelist from Tarsus?"[2]

To be fair, the rejection of the true message of Christmas does not start and end with the Jewish people. Non-Jews are pretty skilled at it as well. As a matter of fact, Jesus Himself predicted that more people would reject Him than accept Him. He reminded us in Matthew's Gospel: "Enter through the narrow gate. For the gate is wide and the road is broad that leads to destruction, and there are many who go through it" (Matthew 7:13, NIV).

Jesus' warning begs a question this Christmas: Why do people reject Him? I mean, His offer of acceptance is pretty amazing, after all. When we receive Him, we get the forgiveness of all our sin, His continued presence in our lives, and the promise of an eternal home in Heaven. And these are just a few of the many promises! Yet many people still reject Jesus. Why?

REASONS PEOPLE REJECT CHRISTMAS AND JESUS

#1 They Don't Believe Jesus Is Who the Bible Says He Is

At the top of the list for why people reject Jesus is that they simply don't believe He is who the Bible says He is. For those in this camp, I present fulfilled prophecies to you!

It might surprise you to learn that first-century Jews also struggled to believe that Jesus was who He said. They were expecting a Messiah but were looking for an entirely different kind. In many regards, they missed the predictions and prophecies about the first coming of Jesus by focusing on the predictions and prophecies about the second coming of Jesus. They were hyper-focused on the Messiah being a powerful, political King. Their preconceived assumptions couldn't accept that the Messiah was born as a baby, lying in a manger. Jesus' arrival didn't carry the type of weight, power, and majesty that they had expected.

I have a very dear friend who is Jewish. We grab lunch almost once a month, play golf, and have even gone to a few football games together. He is an absolutely great guy. Our conversation topics range anywhere from politics, to sports, to family life, and to Jesus. He has yet to profess faith in Jesus alone for salvation, but I believe that day is coming! Over the years, one of the things I've asked him to do is read the book of Revelation and see if the description of the second coming of Jesus could fit the picture of a Messiah for which the vast majority of our Jewish friends have been searching. They simply missed the need for the first coming and fast-forwarded to his second coming.

But whether you are Jewish or not, the sheer number of prophecies fulfilled in the first coming of Jesus should cause you to think about accepting Him as your personal Savior and Lord. Researchers from the article below map it out so well. Let's check it out:

"Some scholars believe that over 300 prophecies from the Old Testament were perfectly fulfilled through the life of the New Testament Jesus. These prophecies were specific enough that the mathematical probability of Jesus fulfilling even a handful of them, let alone all of them, is staggeringly improbable—if not impossible.

Peter Stoner, Chairman of the Departments of Mathematics and Astronomy at Pasadena College, was passionate about biblical prophecies. With 600 students from the InterVarsity Christian Fellowship, Stoner looked at eight specific prophecies about Jesus. They came up with extremely conservative probabilities for each one being fulfilled, and then considered the likelihood of Jesus fulfilling all eight of those prophecies.

The conclusion to his research was staggering. The prospect that anyone would satisfy those eight prophecies was just 1 in 10^{17}. In Science Speaks, he described it like this:

'Let us try to visualize this chance. If you mark one of ten tickets, and place all of the tickets in a hat, and thoroughly stir them, and then ask a blindfolded man to draw one, his chance of getting the right ticket is one in ten. Suppose that we take 10^{17} silver dollars and lay them on the face of Texas. They will cover all of the state two feet deep. Now mark one of these silver dollars and stir the whole mass thoroughly, all over the state.

Blindfold a man and tell him that he can travel as far as he wishes, but he must pick up one silver dollar and say that this is the right one. What chance would he have of getting the right one? Just the same chance that the prophets would have had of writing these eight prophecies and having them all come true in any one man, from their day to the present time, providing they wrote using their own wisdom.'"

The article gives further clarity by mapping out the eight prophecies concerning Jesus' birth and childhood:

"**1. The nations will be blessed through Abraham's leadership.**

Prophecy:

"I will bless those who bless you,
I will curse those who treat you with contempt,
and all the peoples on earth
will be blessed through you." (Genesis 12:3, HCSB)

Fulfillment:

"You are the sons of the prophets and of the covenant that God made with your ancestors, saying to Abraham, And all the families of the earth will be blessed through your offspring. God raised up His Servant and sent Him first to you to bless you by turning each of you from your evil ways." (Acts 3:25-26, HCSB)

2. God's covenant with Isaac's ancestors.

Prophecy:

But God said, "No. Your wife Sarah will bear you a son, and you will name him Isaac. I will confirm My covenant with him as an everlasting covenant for his future offspring. " (Genesis 17:19, HCSB)

Fulfillment:

Neither are they all children because they are Abraham's descendants. On the contrary, your offspring will be traced through Isaac. (Romans 9:7, HCSB)

3. The nations will be blessed through Jacob's offspring.

Prophecy:

"Your offspring will be like the dust of the earth, and you will spread out toward the west, the east, the north, and the south. All the peoples on earth will be blessed through you and your offspring. " (Genesis 28:14, HCSB)

Fulfillment:

Son of Jacob, son of Isaac,
son of Abraham, son of Terah,
son of Nahor... (Luke 3:34, HCSB)

4. The scepter will come through Judah.

Prophecy:

"The scepter will not depart from Judah
or the staff from between his feet
until He whose right it is comes
and the obedience of the peoples belongs to Him. " (Genesis 49:10,

HCSB)

Fulfillment:

son of Amminadab,
son of Ram, son of Hezron,
son of Perez, son of Judah...(Luke 3:33, HCSB)

5. David's offspring will have an eternal kingdom.

Prophecy:

"When your time comes and you rest with your fathers, I will raise
up after you your descendant, who will come from your body, and
I will establish his kingdom. He will build a house for My name,
and I will establish the throne of his kingdom forever." (2 Samuel
7:12-13, HCSB)

Fulfillment:

The historical record of Jesus Christ, the Son of David, the Son of
Abraham... (Matthew 1:1, HCSB)

6. A virgin will give birth, and he will be called Immanuel.

Prophecy:

Therefore, the Lord Himself will give you a sign: The virgin will
conceive, have a son, and name him Immanuel. (Isaiah 7:14,
HCSB)

Fulfillment:

The angel replied to her:

> *"The Holy Spirit will come upon you,*
> *and the power of the Most High will overshadow you.*
> *Therefore, the holy One to be born*
> *will be called the Son of God."* (Luke 1:35, HCSB)

7. The Messiah will end up in Egypt.

Prophecy:

When Israel was a child, I loved him,
and out of Egypt I called My son. (Hosea 11:1, HCSB)

Fulfillment:

So he got up, took the child and His mother during the night, and escaped to Egypt. He stayed there until Herod's death, so that what was spoken by the Lord through the prophet might be fulfilled: Out of Egypt I called My Son. (Matthew 2:14-15, HCSB)

8. The Christ will be born in Bethlehem.

Prophecy:

Bethlehem Ephrathah,
you are small among the clans of Judah;
One will come from you
to be ruler over Israel for Me.
His origin is from antiquity,
from eternity. (Micah 5:2, HCSB)

Fulfillment:

When King Herod heard this, he was deeply disturbed, and all Jerusalem with him. So he assembled all the chief priests and scribes of the people and asked them where the Messiah would be born.

"In Bethlehem of Judea," they told him, "because this is what was written by the prophet:"

> *And you, Bethlehem, in the land of Judah,*
> *are by no means least among the leaders of Judah:*
> *because out of you will come a leader*
> *who will shepherd My people Israel."* (Matthew 2:3-6, HCSB) "[3]

So, for those reluctant to accept Jesus as the Messiah, I present fulfilled prophecy to you.

#2 Some Think They Have Too Much Living to Do

Often you hear people say that they don't want to let Jesus into their lives because *they have too much living to do.* For those that think this way, I present the abundant life that Jesus promises. Here's what Jesus told us:

So Jesus said again, "I assure you: I am the door of the sheep. All who came before Me are thieves and robbers, but the sheep didn't listen to them. I am the door. If anyone enters by Me, he will be saved and will come in and go out and find pasture. A thief comes only to steal and to kill and to destroy. I have come so that they may have life and have it in abundance." (John 10:7-10, HCSB)

Jesus didn't come the first Christmas so that we could sing Christmas carols, decorate our houses, have family gatherings, and buy each other presents. No, He came to bring meaning and purpose to our lives.

I have often heard one of my favorite boyhood preachers, Dr. Jerry Vines, say, "Since I've been saved, I have had more fun on accident than I did on purpose the whole time I was lost." I agree with that. Knowing Jesus is a blast. He promises things like joy, peace, and contentment.

For those who think you have too much living to do before you give your life to Jesus, I would argue exactly the opposite. As a matter of fact, the Bible tells us that we're actually only dead before we meet Jesus. Your life doesn't end when you meet Jesus; your life begins when you meet Jesus.

YOUR LIFE DOESN'T END WHEN YOU MEET JESUS; YOUR LIFE BEGINS WHEN YOU MEET JESUS.

And you were dead in your trespasses and sins in which you previously walked according to the ways of this world, according to the ruler who exercises authority over the lower heavens, the spirit now working in the disobedient. (Ephesians 2:1-2, HCSB)

Being dead doesn't sound like much fun to me. Truthfully, you could not be further from the truth when you reject Jesus because you have too much living to do. You haven't even experienced true life yet. For those of you using this excuse, dive into the full and abundant life that only Jesus Christ can offer!

#3 Some People Think They Could Never Be Good Enough

As a pastor, I've heard this phrase many times over my years in full-time ministry: "I would give my life to Jesus, but I don't think I could ever be good enough." If you've ever felt that way, I present grace to you!

The truth is, people who think that they aren't good enough are right. None of us could ever be *good enough* to deserve eternal life. That's exactly the reason Jesus came in the first place (which we discussed in the last chapter). He offers us the free gift of salvation, and all you have to do is receive it.

As we approach Christmas, I think sharing my *Christmas Gift Policy* may be helpful to you at this point. I have a straightforward rule when someone gives me a gift during the days leading up to Christmas. I open it and start using it right away. If you give me a gift on December 15th, I don't wait until Christmas Day to unpackage it. Here's my reasoning: I believe the highest form of appreciation when someone is kind enough to give you a gift is to receive it and use it.

Christmas comes, and with it is the gift of eternal life that Jesus brought with Him. The highest form of appreciation for that gift is to receive the Christ of Christmas into your heart—right away and without delay!

MAKING ROOM

Yes, Christmas comes, and some reject it. But that doesn't have to be your story. While some reject Him, many also choose to accept Him.

He was in the world,
and the world was created through Him,
yet the world did not recognize Him.

He came to His own,
and His own people did not receive Him.
But to all who did receive Him,
He gave them the right to be children of God,
to those who believe in His name... (John 1:10-12, HCSB)

One of my favorite Christmas stories is about an oversized little boy named Johnny who was asked to play the innkeeper in the annual Christmas program for his school. Poor Johnny looked like he was in seventh grade, although he was only in third. However, the size of Johnny's heart matched the size of his frame.

The time came for the Christmas program, and Johnny had memorized his one line: "No room." During the show, a little pregnant Mary and Joseph walked on stage, and they knocked on the innkeeper's door in the middle of the night. Johnny heard the knocking and opened the door, just like they had practiced. However, he appeared to be speechless when it was time to say his line. It was shocking since he only had two words to remember: "No room."

The teachers thought he had forgotten the line. So, they began whispering the line from the side of the stage: "No room, Johnny. No room. No room. No room. That's your only line. No room." But Johnny hadn't forgotten the line. He just didn't have the heart to say it. Finally, he threw a major wrench in the rest of the Christmas play when he blurted out, "Oh shucks, you guys come on in here. I'll go outside."

I love it when people like Johnny decide to make room for Jesus in their lives. Over the years, I've had a front-row seat to seeing people just like him choose to make room in their hearts for Jesus as they become a follower. Can I challenge you this Christmas to set aside the excuses and make room for Christmas to come into your life like never before? Say yes to Jesus, who already said yes to you so many years ago when He was born in a manger, lived a sinless life, and died on Calvary's cross for you.

If you're ready to say yes to Jesus, would you pray this prayer with me, right where you are?

"Jesus, I ask you to come into my heart and forgive me for my sin. I believe that You died on the cross so that I could be forgiven. I accept Your sacrifice and a relationship with You. I commit my life to You today and forever and ever. Amen."

If you prayed that prayer, I'm so proud of you! I also want to encourage you to let someone know about it who can help you on your journey with Jesus. Tell your friends and family. Find a church where you can share this with one of the pastors. And also, let me know: text "ISAIDYES" to 94000.

REFLECTION QUESTIONS

1. Have you been around people who reject Christmas for one reason or another? How did you respond to their lack of enthusiasm about the gift of Jesus coming to live among us?

2. Are there times when you feel like putting your relationship with Jesus on the back burner because you want to live your way instead of God's way? Are you ready to fully surrender to His will and plans for your life?

3. What sin or circumstance have you allowed the enemy to use to convince you that you are not good enough to experience life in Jesus? Can you imagine what your life would be like if you made room for Jesus, laid your shame down at His feet, and experienced the fullness of His love for you this Christmas?

CHAPTER 5

CHRISTMAS COMES AND CHANGES EVERYTHING

The lyrics of *Christmas Changes Everything*, written by Josh Wilson, truly capture the essence of the life-changing effect Christmas can have on us all:

"O Holy night, starry sky
We were dead until tonight
Christmas changes everything

Long lay the world inside our sin
He has come here to forgive
Christmas changes everything

Hallelujah, love has found us
Hope in a manger our Saviour is setting us free
This is rescue, Christ has come to make us new
Oh Christmas changes everything

Now God has met us where we are
A thrill of hope for hopeless hearts
His perfect love will shatter every fear

We're coming back to life again
And it's all because of Bethlehem
Rejoice, oh rejoice!

Hallelujah, love has found us
Hope in a manger our Saviour is setting us free
This is rescue, Christ has come to make us new
Oh Christmas changes everything

We will fall on our knees
We will fall on our knees
We will fall on our knees

O Holy night, holy child
We were dead till you came to life

Hallelujah, you have found us
Hope in a manger, oh Saviour we fall on our knees
You are rescue, you are making all things new
Oh Christmas changes everything
Yeah Christmas changes everything
Christmas changes everything."[1]

Say it or sing it with me: "Christmas changes everything!" Christmas is a time for celebration, and not just because we successfully made it to the end of another crazy year. When Jesus came to our broken world in human flesh, He changed everything. And because of that, He can also change everything about your life.

Let's look back at the narrative of Christmas. God made us—human beings—in His image. Adam and Eve experienced a perfect reality in the Garden of Eden. They had everything they could ever desire, lacking nothing whatsoever. Most importantly, they had unrestricted access to God. They enjoyed the kind of intimacy with the Almighty that we can only dream about!

However, Adam and Eve chose to disobey God by eating the fruit He forbade, and in turn invited sin to ruin the perfect reality of Eden. As a result, their joy was replaced by trials and suffering. Worst of all, their unrestricted access and deep intimacy with God were forfeited through one act of disobedience. At that moment, humanity chose evil lies over God's truth, and we became a people without hope—a world needing to be saved.

Yet God had a plan. Remember that *fullness of time* talk we had during chapter one? In the fullness of time, Jesus changed everything and everyone who believed in Him.

- In the life of a young teenage woman named Mary—Jesus changed everything.
- In the life of twelve ordinary men—Jesus changed everything.
- In the life of a woman caught in adultery—Jesus changed everything.
- In the life of a Pharisee who was filled with hate and murder—Jesus changed everything.

But get this: He didn't change their past—He changed their hearts. Jesus doesn't give us new lives, He makes our lives new. When He starts to work in our lives light overtakes darkness, joy overcomes sadness, healing overwhelms our brokenness, and truth obliterates lies. In the end, love really does conquer all.

JESUS DOESN'T GIVE US NEW LIVES, HE MAKES OUR LIVES NEW.

As you read this book today, it is some 2,000 years after the birth of Jesus. Even so, He is still working in our world. The fact that Jesus is still changing everything is a cause for celebration!

In the previous chapter, we talked about how many people rejected Jesus. My call to action was an invitation to accept Jesus if you hadn't done so already. Some of you might have been wondering: Jackie, *what happens when I start a relationship with Jesus?* Well, I'm glad you asked! Let's take a deep dive into the benefits of welcoming Jesus into your life. If you already have a relationship with Jesus, this will encourage you to keep your eyes on Him. If you are thinking about starting that relationship, I pray this will motivate you to make the most important decision ever—to give your life to Jesus and allow

Him to change you.

One of my favorite Bible verses is 2 Corinthians 5:17: "Therefore, if anyone is in Christ, he is a new creation; old things have passed away, and look, new things have come" (HCSB). What are some of those new things, or benefits, Jesus can bring to your life? There are four catchwords that capture the heart of Jesus' arrival on Christmas. These four words are also the essence of the change Christ wants to bring to our hearts and lives. He transforms us into people of *peace*, *joy*, *love*, and *hope*.

The back of this book includes an Advent Devotional Guide that centers around the study of these four words. But for now, let's explore how Jesus wants to mark us with peace, joy, love, and hope. After all, who couldn't use more of those characteristics?! Here's how Christmas, or the arrival of Christ, brings these attributes to fullness in our lives.

FOUR WAYS CHRISTMAS CHANGES EVERYTHING

#1 Peace

When the Old Testament prophet Micah predicted the first Christmas, he foresaw the promise of peace that would come with it:

Now, daughter who is under attack,
you slash yourself in grief;
a siege is set against us!
They are striking the judge of Israel
on the cheek with a rod.
Bethlehem Ephrathah,
you are small among the clans of Judah;
One will come from you
to be ruler over Israel for Me.

His origin is from antiquity,
from eternity.
Therefore, He will abandon them until the time
when she who is in labor has given birth;
then the rest of His brothers will return
to the people of Israel.
He will stand and shepherd them
in the strength of Yahweh,
in the majestic name of Yahweh His God.
They will live securely,
for then His greatness will extend
to the ends of the earth.
He will be their peace.
When Assyria invades our land,
when it marches against our fortresses,
we will raise against it seven shepherds,
even eight leaders of men. (Micah 5:1-5, HCSB)

Over 700 years before Jesus' arrival, Micah prophesied that He would be our peace. And that first Christmas night, the angels confirmed the prediction of Jesus' peace to the shepherds keeping watch over their flocks:

Suddenly there was a multitude of the heavenly host with the
angel, praising God and saying:

"Glory to God in the highest heaven, and peace on earth to
people He favors!" (Luke 2:13-14, HCSB)

One of the ways Jesus changes everything is by bringing peace to a world at war with God and others. Perhaps that is best illustrated in the story of missionaries Don and Carol Richardson:

"In 1962, Don and his wife Carol moved to West Papua, Indonesia. With their 6-month-old son Steve in their arms, the Richardsons approached the Sawi tribe, not realizing that the very act of carrying their infant was a sign of peace to the 400 Sawi waiting to greet them.

As the Richardsons began to explain Jesus' story to the tribe, they realized that the Sawi were interpreting Jesus' betrayer Judas as the hero of the story. It turned out the Sawi idealized treachery. Sometimes they would even befriend a member of another village for the sole purpose of later betraying him to the death and having a cannibalistic feast.

In time, battles broke out between various villages over who got to be close to the Richardsons. When Don told them they needed to make peace or they would leave, a man brought his baby son to another tribe. The Richardsons were told that in the Sawi community, when one village wanted to make peace, they presented one of their children to another village. For as long as that 'peace child' lived, there would be peace between the enemies.

After working hard to explain the Good News, Carol Richardson finally realized that this 'peace child' act was a metaphor for the Gospel. A father would give his son to the enemy to restore peace and bring reconciliation.

After this 'peace child' explanation of the Gospel, says Steve, 'There was a breakthrough among the Sawi. They started recognizing that Jesus was God's peace child—the ultimate peace child.'

'They began responding to the Gospel, and the Sawi eventually began reaching out in their own missionary efforts to tribes they had previously warred against,' Steve adds."[2]

As we celebrate the ultimate *peace child* this Christmas, we understand that there would be no peace without Him. There are a few specific ways that He brings peace to our lives. First, Christmas brings *peace with God.*

This is the one truth of the holidays that serves as the foundation for our worship of God. We celebrate the birth of Jesus, first and foremost, because He has brought peace between God and us.

You might be thinking: *But God and me are cool. I don't have a problem with Him. Why would He have any problem with me?*

Maybe you can resonate with the story of a man bedridden in the hospital. This man, who was close to death, received a visit from a minister who asked him, "Have you made your peace with God?"

The man responded: "I didn't know we had ever quarreled."

Many people in the world feel the exact same way as the man in this story. However, Jesus brought us the opportunity to make peace with God by laying down His life for us so that we could be reunited with our creator. In fact, without a relationship with this child of peace, we are at war with God. That's what the Apostle Paul says in his letter to Ephesus:

> So then, remember that at one time you were Gentiles in the
> flesh—called "the uncircumcised" by those called "the circumcised,"
> which is done in the flesh by human hands. At that time you
> were without the Messiah, excluded from the citizenship of Israel,
> and foreigners to the covenants of the promise, without hope and
> without God in the world. But now in Christ Jesus, you who were
> far away have been brought near by the blood of the Messiah. For
> He is our peace, who made both groups one and tore down the
> dividing wall of hostility. (Ephesians 2:12-14, HCSB)

What a gift this is to us. We who were far from God, even enemies against Him because of sin, are now at peace with Him through the work of His Son. Jesus is the bridge that connects imperfect people with a perfect God! And when that happens, it not only brings outer peace but much needed inner peace.

JESUS IS THE BRIDGE THAT CONNECTS IMPERFECT PEOPLE WITH A PERFECT GOD!

Not only does Christmas bring us peace with God, it also brings us the *peace of God*. The Christmas season is likely the most pressing time of the year when we need the peace of God in our hearts the most. During this season, the busyness of life tends to wage war against our inner-calm. The only remedy is the peace that only Jesus brings. It is a welcome relief from the chaos of the season.

The Bible tells us in Philippians 4:7, "And the peace of God, which surpasses every thought, will guard your hearts and minds in Christ Jesus" (HCSB).

The peace of God stands like a centurion at the gate of our hearts and minds to keep us steady in an unsteady world. Jesus' peace combats our uncertain thoughts and keeps us grounded in Him. From now on, whenever you think of Christmas, I hope that one of the first words you think of is *peace*. The peace that came packaged with Christ on Christmas changes everything. Jesus' gift giving doesn't end with His offering of peace, He also extends the gift of joy to each one of us.

#2 Joy

Isaac Watts captured the arrival of joy in his famous hymn, *Joy to the World*:

"Joy to the world! The Lord is come
Let earth receive her King!
Let every heart prepare Him room
And heaven and nature sing."[3]

There is a certain sadness and heaviness that settles in on a world that is void of Christ. This fact is true today and it was certainly true in the first century leading up to the arrival of the Christ Child. Remember the 400 years of silence between the Old Testament and Jesus' arrival? Remember Herod's rule and the hopelessness of living under the heavy hand of a tyrant? Someone living in that era wouldn't have many reasons to be joyful. But that's when Jesus burst onto the scene of humanity and gave us all a cause for joy. It made such an impact on the shepherds who held baby Jesus on that first Christmas that they "returned, glorifying and praising God for all the things they had seen and heard, just as they had been told" (Luke 2:20, HCSB).

Before the arrival of Jesus, the shepherds were likely sucked into the same vortex of sadness as the rest of Israel which was void of God's voice. But one moment in the presence of their Savior produced so much joy that they left the experience praising God. Today, people that choose to live their lives apart from Jesus are consumed with a similar sadness. They may attempt masking the sadness with relationships, exotic vacations, material possessions, or wild parties. However, beneath the surface of those empty solutions is discontented joylessness. Consider the words of comedian and television star Jerry Seinfeld: "Everybody's looking for good sex, good food, and a good laugh. They're little islands of relief in what's often a painful existence."[4]

Sadly, the world people live in apart from Christ is a *painful existence*. It leaves them seeking elusive joy in trips of personal pleasure that never fully satisfy. As Joy Davidman says, "Living for his own pleasure is the least pleasurable thing a man can do; if his neighbors don't kill him in disgust, he will die slowly of boredom and powerlessness."[5]

Depressed yet? Thankfully, here comes the good part! Jesus' arrival replaced sadness with joy. When we invite Him into our lives, He gives us a deep, ever-abiding joy that the world cannot steal. Did you know that the words *joy, rejoice*, or *joyful* appear over 400 times in the Bible? God repeats the things that are important to Him! He wants you to have joy.

As a matter of fact, Jesus said, "Until now you have not asked for anything in my name. Ask and you will receive, and your joy will be complete" (John 16:24, NIV). Furthermore, I love the words of the psalmist in the Old Testament when he wrote: "You reveal the path of life to me; in Your presence is abundant joy; in Your right hand are eternal pleasures" (Psalms 16:11, HCSB)

Looking for joy this Christmas? Look to Jesus!

"Friends all around us are trying to find
What the heart yearns for, by sin undermined;
I have the secret, I know where 'tis found:
Only in Jesus true pleasures (joy) abound."[6]

#3 Love

Jesus entered into a world of hate and preached a message of love. As a matter of fact, the entire reason behind Jesus coming to us was the love of God. The sweetest Christmas verse in the Bible is found in John 3:16: "For God so loved the world that he gave his one and only Son" (NIV). The fuel that drives Christmas is the love of God. He loves you so much that He came to earth as a human so you could get to know Him, learn to trust Him, and love Him back. Theologians call the arrival of Jesus the incarnation. It's a fancy term that explains how Jesus invaded the history of mankind in the most significant way our world has ever seen.

I love how Rick Warren describes it in his classic book, *The Purpose of Christmas:* "One potential problem of our annual Christmas celebrations is that many people only think of Jesus as a baby! Their conception of Him is only as a helpless newborn in His mother's arms. If Jesus had never grown up to do what He did, He'd have no power to transform our lives. But the baby born in Bethlehem did not stay a baby. Jesus grew to manhood, modeled for us the kind of life that pleases God, taught us the truth, paid for every sin we commit by dying on a cross, then proved that He was God and could save us by coming back to life. This is the Good News. When the Romans nailed Jesus to a cross, they stretched His arms as wide as they could. With his arms wide open, Jesus was physically demonstrating, 'I love you this much! I love you so much it hurts! I'd rather die than live without you!' The next time you see a picture or statue of Jesus with outstretched arms on the cross, remember, He is saying, "I love you this much!"[7]

Jesus' arrival on Christmas is God saying to each one of us: "I love you", and that one simple truth changes everything. Have you ever received the love of God personally? Have you ever stepped inside the circle of God's unconditional love for you? If not, then why not now? Accept His love and forgiveness and watch him change you from the inside out. If you feel distant from a loving God, what you need is a personal incarnation. It is not enough for you to only believe that Jesus invaded history as a baby born in Bethlehem. Jesus wants to invade your life and see you born again by believing and trusting in Him!

#4 Hope

One of the most powerful realities that Christmas brings is hope. Christmas provides us hope even when we are living in darkness. The truth is, darkness is where light actually shines the brightest! That's the heart of the Christmas story—an overriding message of hope. Jesus, who had no darkness in Him at all, entered into our darkness to change our narrative. This idea is articulated beautifully in the lyrics of *O Holy Night*: "O holy night, the stars are brightly shining, it is the night of our dear Savior's birth."[8] God didn't plan His entrance into our world for high noon. Fittingly, He entered into the darkness—showing us the way to light, guiding us towards hope, and demonstrating how to overcome the shadows of our own evil. Christmas teaches us that we can have hope in Jesus' everlasting light even when things seem dark.

Christmas reminds us that if Jesus came once, He will surely come again. He came that first Christmas because He has eternal plans for us. Christmas came, and Jesus is coming again. He is not going to leave us in a world without hope. We have something and someone to look forward to. We can believe in the second coming of Christ when He will restore the earth to His perfect original intention. His return from heaven will be personal, visible, and glorious—a blessed hope for which we should constantly watch and pray.

And if you think Christmas changes everything, just wait until the second coming of Christ. That will change everything in a way that we have never seen before!

Then I saw a new heaven and a new earth, for the first heaven and the first earth had passed away, and the sea no longer existed. I also saw the Holy City, new Jerusalem, coming down out of heaven from God, prepared like a bride adorned for her husband.

Then I heard a loud voice from the throne:

> *"Look! God's dwelling is with humanity,*
> *and He will live with them.*
> *They will be His people,*
> *and God Himself will be with them*
> *and be their God.*
> *He will wipe away every tear from their eyes.*
> *Death will no longer exist;*
> *grief, crying, and pain will exist no longer,*
> *because the previous things have passed away."*

Then the One seated on the throne said, "Look! I am making everything new." He also said, "Write, because these words are faithful and true." (Revelation 21:1-5, HCSB)

Real hope is not found in comfortable circumstances or favorable outcomes. It is not found in earthly relationships or affections. Sooner or later, everything on this planet that we place our hope in will disappoint us. The only one that can truly give us real hope goes by the name of Jesus. He is perfectly loving, kind, understanding, just, fair, and compassionate. Jesus invites us to journey past the temporary and place our hope in something much more valuable— the eternal! He is not only restoring humanity, He is restoring us personally. And His restoration has no end.

Christmas is more than a baby's arrival in a manger that we contemplate once a year. Christmas is the vehicle of hope that changes everything about our lives and future. Christmas is clear proof of God's individual and personal love to each one of us. It gives us the opportunity to experience incredible joy despite the circumstances or situations we may be facing in our world. It overwhelms us with a sense of peace that we can't understand, but desperately need. Christmas changes everything!

REFLECTION QUESTIONS

1. How have you experienced Jesus changing everything in your life?

2. What imperfections in your life do you need Jesus to remove this Christmas so that you can be united with our perfect God?

3. What gift of Jesus do you need to embrace and allow to impact your life? How can the peace, joy, love, and hope of Christmas change your life today?

CHAPTER 6

CHRISTMAS COMES AND WE SHOULD DECLARE IT

"Go, tell it on the mountain
Over the hills and everywhere
Go, tell it on the mountain
That Jesus Christ is born."[1]

No discussion of Christmas would be complete without a challenge to declare the good news it brings to the entire world. Christmas is not a secret to keep, it is a message to share. Sharing this message of peace, joy, love, and hope can change people's lives. Remember the movie *The Grinch?* When Cindy Lou Who shared the hope of Christmas with the green Grinch, his heart grew three sizes that day.

CHRISTMAS IS NOT A SECRET TO KEEP, IT IS A MESSAGE TO SHARE.

We live in a *grinchy* world. It's a world filled with Grinches and Scrooges that need the hope of Christmas like never before. And when we share the real message of Christmas with others, it will do more than grow the size of their heart; it will change them from the inside out.

When Baby Jesus was dedicated at the temple, a prophet named Simeon declared the special place in history that He would have:

Simeon took Him up in his arms, praised God, and said:

"Now, Master,
You can dismiss Your slave in peace,
as You promised.

For my eyes have seen Your salvation.
You have prepared it
in the presence of all peoples—
a light for revelation to the Gentiles
and glory to Your people Israel. " (Luke 2:28-32, HCSB)

Just moments later, the prophetess Anna also declared the glory of the Christ Child:

At that very moment, she came up and began to thank God
and to speak about Him to all who were looking forward to the
redemption of Jerusalem. (Luke 2:38, HCSB)

Even heaven itself declared the supremacy of Jesus as the world watched at His baptism:

When all the people were baptized, Jesus also was baptized. As He
was praying, heaven opened, and the Holy Spirit descended on
Him in a physical appearance like a dove. And a voice came from
heaven:

> *"You are My beloved Son.*
> *I take delight in You!"* (Luke 3:21-22, HCSB)

Jesus has called us to model the example of those declarations. After His earthly ministry, before He left our planet and ascended back into heaven, these were His instructions:

He said to them, "It is not for you to know times or periods that
the Father has set by His own authority. But you will receive
power when the Holy Spirit has come on you, and you will be My
witnesses in Jerusalem, in all Judea and Samaria, and to the ends
of the earth. " (Acts 1:7-8, HCSB)

FOR JESUS-FOLLOWERS, DECLARING HIM TO THE WORLD IS NOT A SUBTLE SUGGESTION; IT IS A DIVINE COMMANDMENT.

For Jesus-followers, declaring Him to the world is not a subtle suggestion; it is a divine commandment. And Christmas offers us an amazing opportunity to do just that.

So, stop worrying about whether people are saying "Merry Christmas" or "happy holidays." Don't lose sleep over the kind of cup a certain coffee shop is pouring your morning joe into. Those things don't make a lasting impact on anyone's eternity! Jesus never said: "After the Holy Spirit comes upon you, you will say 'Merry Christmas,' and drink coffee from cups that say the same." The hope of Christmas is so much bigger than that! We are to become His witnesses—spreading the Gospel message that can change lives and alter the world. Whether you just received Jesus into your life or you have known Him for years, God can use your witness to impact people in ways that you could never imagine. Ezekiel says that when someone receives the Lord, He will, "Give you a new heart and put a new spirit in you; I will remove from you your heart of stone and give you a heart of flesh" (Ezekiel 36:26, HCSB).

God transplanting a brand-new heart for someone is better than an old, dead heart *growing three sizes* in a day. God gives hearts that are loving toward Him, loving toward others, at peace with their past, and excited for their future.

Christmas comes. When it does, we have a responsibility to share the real meaning of it with others. Fortunately, Christmas is one of the holidays where engaging others in a Gospel conversation is more natural than other times of the year. It's the time of year when we share laughter, food, and, of course, gifts. Maybe this Christmas, it's time to give your family, friends, neighbors, work associates, classmates, or even complete strangers the greatest Christmas gift ever—the message of Jesus Christ.

There is no better gift than the Good News of Jesus. He truly is the reason for the season! Think about it. After you meet Jesus, you are now privy to the most crucial message in the world. If you currently know Jesus, you currently have top-secret clearance to the world's best news. You understand how sins are forgiven, how to live in Jesus' presence daily, and the assurance of an eternal home. Furthermore, you have successfully avoided eternity separated from God in hell. You have the opportunity to invite family, friends, co-workers, and even strangers to the same experience! What kind of person would you be if you decided not to share this eternity-transforming reality with others?

Let's think about it another way. If you came across the cure for cancer but didn't share it with a hurting world, your actions would be considered criminal at the very least. Let's pretend like you discovered a cure for Covid in the early days of 2020 but chose to keep it a secret. Your secrecy would make you indirectly guilty for over four million worldwide deaths and counting as I'm writing this.

Here's our spiritual reality: The world is sick with a much greater illness than cancer or Covid. They are sick with the disease of sin. The end result of sin, when it is left untreated, is eternal death, and separation from God.

This is why Paul says that "the wages of sin is death" (Romans 6:23, HCSB). That's pretty depressing news. However, Jesus came as the cure to our terminal sin problem. In the very same verse, Paul shares the remedy to death when he says, "but the gift of God is eternal life in Christ Jesus our Lord" (Romans 6:23, HCSB). That's why the Gospel is known as the Good News!

5 WAYS TO DECLARE CHRISTMAS...PLUS ONE

I want to challenge you to look for powerful and creative ways to share Jesus with others this Christmas season. All of us have a responsibility to leverage our lives in order to introduce the lost to the Lord.

I recently read a wonderful article by Greg Stier on the *Church Leaders* website. It really captured God's heart by giving practical ways to leverage the Christmas season and share the message of Jesus with a lost world. As you read through, think of how you might be able to take action in your context.

"Here are are five simple ways to share Christ this Christmas:

1. Invite another family to go with you to Christmas Eve services and use it as a Gospel conversation starter.

If there's ever a time people are pre-conditioned to go to church, it's on Christmas Eve. The Christmas story becomes an excellent entry point to the Gospel message. Maybe have them over for some eggnog afterward and ask a question like, "So why do you think the story of Jesus' birth is so important to so many churches?" or "What was the most meaningful part of the service to you?" Both of these questions can become a jumping off point for a deeper Gospel conversation.

2. Write someone a personal letter that explains the Gospel in the context of Christmas.

There's nothing more powerful than a hand-written, heartfelt letter. A letter is both personal and permanent (because typically people don't throw hand-written letters away!). The entire book of John was a hand-written letter primarily written to those who had not yet believed in Jesus. That's why the Apostle wrote, "These things were written that you might believe that Jesus is the Son of God and that by believing you may have life through his name" (John 20:31, NIV).

At some point, you can make the *salvation segue* with a phrase like, "During this Christmas season I cannot help but be thinking of you and how much you mean to me. Because you mean so much I wanted to share something that means the most to me...my relationship with Jesus."

3. Send someone a link to a short video that clearly shares the Gospel.

There are many great videos that can be used to share the good news of Jesus this holiday season. Here are just a few:

* Life in Six Words... This spoken word piece from Propaganda is clear, compelling and, well, very cool. It is truly a viral video that millions of believers and nonbelievers alike have seen. Check it out at www.lifein6words.com.
* Falling Plates... This is a visually stunning presentation of the Good News that will be sure to capture people's attention. Check it out at www.fallingplates.com.
* Something Amazing... This animated presentation of the Gospel is short and sweet (two minutes) but gets the job done! Check it out www.somethingamazing.net.

4. Have a meal and movie night.

Invite some family, friends, or neighbors over for a meal and movie night. You could start with a funny one (*A Christmas*

Story?) and follow it up with a movie that could spark a Gospel conversation over hot cocoa (*The Nativity Story?*).

There's nothing like a meal together and a few laughs to open the door for a deeper conversation about the thing that matters most...our relationship with Jesus!

5. Just have the conversation.

Not to be too simplistic but maybe, just maybe, it's time to just bring it up. Ask the person God has placed on your heart where they are spiritually, what their view of God is and what they think about this whole "Jesus thing." After all, it's Christmas. His Name is central to the celebration.
Then, after you listen to them deeply, share with them honestly about why you're a Christian. Be upfront about how much Jesus means to you."[2]

It wouldn't be right if I didn't shamelessly add one other strategy for sharing Christ this Christmas season: **Share your copy of *Christmas Comes* with someone.**

I hope you have found that this little book is stuffed full of the Gospel. It even has numerous invitations for readers to give their life to Christ. Why? Because Christmas comes, whether people are ready or not.

The real Christmas arrived with inexplicable force. Nothing could stop it. Not Herod, the forces of Rome, the Pharisees, or taxation and travel difficulties. It came with the stealth-like accuracy of a Navy SEAL team on a top-secret mission.

But what if I told you Christmas can come to people today with the same force and precision that it did 2000 years ago? What if our faith was big enough to believe that Jesus still shows up in people's lives unexpectedly?

Today, some people coast through life with no expectation that Jesus might interrupt their regularly scheduled programming to shock their spiritual system from death to life. What if God used you to provide that shock? What if He's asking you to surprise someone this Christmas with Jesus' message of hope?

What if Jesus showed up today in the middle of chaos? So many people are far from God, hurting and living empty lives. Times of tension are when Jesus does His best work. He has a way of showing up and bringing light to dark places. That's why we should remain prayerful about sharing the Gospel with people around us. When we see someone going through difficulty, our spiritual radar should alert us that it's a good time to share the hope of Jesus.

But Jackie, what if I approach the wrong person? Impossible! Everybody needs Jesus. I'm convinced there are no accidental conversations about the Gospel. We all need more of Jesus because we have all sinned and fallen short of God's plan for our lives.

Sharing Jesus with others and watching Him transform them is the greatest joy of life. What an honor to play a small part in someone's journey from darkness to light, hopelessness to hope, and from death to eternal life.

This is why we should declare the coming of Christmas! Maybe through the declaration of this book, God has spoken to you. Maybe you've decided for the first time to give your life to Jesus. Don't forget to declare it. You don't have to be an expert to let somebody else know!

Here's what Jesus told us about declaring Him to the world around us: "Therefore, everyone who will acknowledge Me before men, I will also acknowledge him before My Father in heaven. But whoever denies Me before men, I will also deny him before My Father in heaven" (Matthew 10:32-33, HCSB) My prayer is that since declaration is so important to Jesus, it also becomes important to you.

Maybe the Good News of Christmas has touched you deeply

through this book. You might feel inspired to share with the world, but you don't know Jesus for yourself yet. The first step, which you can take right now, is starting a relationship with Him. If you are ready for Him to change everything, then please let us know about it. Text "ISAIDYES" to 94000, and we will give you some next steps to help you start walking with Jesus. Also, I'd encourage you to find a local church. Tell the pastor about your decision, and get connected with other believers that can help you grow.

In conclusion, it's true that "Christmas comes but once a year, and when it comes, it brings great cheer." So, from my heart to yours, Merry Christmas!

REFLECTION QUESTIONS

1. When was the last time that you shared the message of Jesus with someone during the Christmas season?

2. Who do you need to declare the truth of Christmas to today? Who are you praying for that needs to hear about the hope of Jesus during this Christmas season?

3. After reading this book, what action is God calling you to? How do you need to live differently because of the truth that you have learned throughout the pages of *Christmas Comes*?

ADVENT DEVOTIONAL

WRITTEN & COMPILED BY
ANDREW BAILEY

Advent refers to the weeks that lead up to Christmas. Traditionally, it's a time when Christians prayerfully reflect on the birth of Jesus and what it means to their life. My prayer is that this Advent Devotional helps you to experience the greatest Christmas ever, not because of presents or parties, but because of the hopeful, eternal, and transformational reality of Jesus.

HOPE BECAUSE OF HIS COMING

PEACE THROUGH HIS KINGDOM

LOVE SHOWN BY HIS PROMISES

JOY FROM HIS PRESENCE

SALVATION IS HERE

DECEMBER 1
LOST MY RESTING PLACE

My people are lost sheep; their shepherds led them astray, guiding them the wrong way in the mountains. They wandered from mountain to hill; they forgot their resting place. (Jeremiah 50:6, HCSB)

The Christmas season seems to be about anything but rest. As soon as the calendar flips to December, the countdown to Christmas begins. Between buying presents, planning parties, coordinating schedules, and dreading the family visits to come—Christmas can feel like a time of chaos that we just aren't prepared for. All of the busyness and noise around the holiday season are like "shepherds" leading us astray. We become like lost sheep in a season that carries so much significance.

So, what is Christmas really all about? It is summed up beautifully in Luke 19:10: "For the Son of Man has come to seek and to save the lost" (NIV). The advent season is all about God finding His people who have wandered away, who are focused on the wrong priorities, who stopped looking for Him, who aren't expecting Him to show up, and who are tired and burned out. The "lost" are the people He invites to welcome Him as their Savior.

When Jesus began His ministry through teaching, He quickly revealed His purpose in Matthew 11:28: "Come to me, all of you who are weary and burdened, and I will give you rest"(NIV). It's easy to fall into the trap of chaos and busyness during Christmas, but my prayer is that as this season begins, we are drawn to look to Christ and find our resting place.

Further Reading: Isaiah 2:2-5

WHAT IS GOD TEACHING ME TO BE, THINK, OR DO TODAY...

DECEMBER 2
PREPARING MYSELF FOR THE KING

Therefore, Israel, that is what I will do to you, and since I will do that to you, Israel, prepare to meet your God! (Amos 4:12, HCSB)

Have you ever hosted family members at Christmas? The preparation process always seems to be full of stress: cleaning the house, buying the food, and finding and putting out the décor that your in-laws bought you last Christmas. However, despite all of the stress, we still jump into all of that work willingly. The payoff of spending time with our loved ones is worth it.

So, why is it so easy to spiritually neglect Jesus when we know He is coming? When Jesus received criticism saying that He wasn't speaking on behalf of God, He gave a way to test motives in John 7:17: "If anyone wants to do His will, he will know whether the teaching is from God or whether I am speaking on my own" (HCSB). We often ignore Jesus during the chaos of Christmas because we are focused on our will instead of His.

When we step back, it's ironic how much we stress over preparing a Christmas meal, but aren't too concerned over preparing for our King. This Advent season, I pray that we can all stop and recognize the weightiness of God. John Piper describes it this way: "You are the Christ, the Son of the living God, the consolation of my past, the redemption of my future. Now I see you. Now I receive you—for who you really are."[1]

Further Reading: Isaiah 9:1-7

WHAT IS GOD TEACHING ME TO BE, THINK, OR DO TODAY...

DECEMBER 3
HOPE FOR MY FUTURE, DESPITE MY PAST

Look, I am about to do something new; even now it is coming. Do you not see it? Indeed, I will make a way in the wilderness, rivers in the desert. (Isaiah 43:19, HCSB)

One of the biggest thieves of holiday joy during the Christmas season is the past. All of us have a past, and holidays can be the breeding grounds for painful memories to resurface year after year. A common reaction to this past hurt and pain is to put your head down and hope the season passes quickly.

However, that's not the hope Jesus brought on Christmas, and it's not how God deals with the past. When Israel was continually unfaithful, God could have erased the past and started with a new nation. Instead, He dealt with the past as stated by Matthew 1:17: "So all the generations from Abraham to David were 14 generations; and from David until the exile to Babylon, 14 generations; and from the exile to Babylon until the Messiah, 14 generations" (HCSB).

Before Jesus, Isaiah tells us that Israel's many generations were a "stump," but Jesus was a "branch" that "bears fruit" (Isaiah 11:1). What does this mean? Because of Jesus, our past does nothing to limit our future. He can take a dead stump and turn it into a beautiful tree that bears greater fruit than we could ever imagine. Paul tells us in 2 Corinthians 5:17: "Therefore, if anyone is in Christ, he is a new creation; the old has passed away, and see, the new has come!" (CSB). God doesn't hold our past against us; rather He forgives us for everything we have done, He heals us from the pain that we have endured, and He gives us hope for the future to come! Let's pray that God releases any burden of our past this Advent season.

Further Reading: Isaiah 11:1-9

WHAT IS GOD TEACHING ME TO BE, THINK, OR DO TODAY...

DECEMBER 4
KINGDOM-TRADITION BEFORE MY OWN

But to all who did receive Him, He gave them the right to be children of God, to those who believe in His name, who were born, not of natural descent, or of the will of the flesh, or of the will of man, but of God. (John 1:12-13, HCSB)

The holiday season brings an abundance of traditions: from religious ones like Christmas, Hanukkah, and Kwanza to cultural ones like tamales, eggnog, cookies for Santa, and those personal to each family. These traditions either lead to celebration or resentment. Celebrations happen through forging new memories with family and friends that remember the past. Resentments occur when you walk through the motions of a tradition that you may not welcome anymore. Yet, that's not what Christmas is about. It's not about an ode to the past or history that is disconnected and irrelevant from your current life. Instead, it's a reminder of why God saved us and the significance of our true family.

John explained that we were given the right to become God's children because of His grace, not traditions or the past. As a part of this new family, we are given a new Kingdom-tradition in which we must continue to participate. Paul explains how it should look in Romans 14:17: "...for the kingdom of God is not eating and drinking, but righteousness, peace, and joy in the Holy Spirit" (HCSB). Likewise, Isaiah had a vision of the future where Jesus would be the banner of hope for all nations. Still, only the remnant of His people would find that "his resting place will be glorious" (Isaiah 11:10, HCSB). I pray that in this season, we don't get lost in our own earthly traditions. My hope is that we all prioritize the family traditions of our Father in heaven. (**Further Reading:** Isaiah 11:10-16)

WHAT IS GOD TEACHING ME TO BE, THINK, OR DO TODAY...

DECEMBER 5
MY SINS DON'T STOP GOD

The counsel of the Lord stands forever, the plans of His heart from generation to generation. (Psalm 33:11, HCSB)

Christmas can be one of most intimidating times of the entire year for parents. Their minds can easily be flooded with questions like: *Will the kids like their presents? Will they get their share of lights, snow, carolers, etc? Will they act civilized when the family comes over? Will we create happy memories that start traditions or sad ones that create scars?* There is a natural pressure to make sure a positive family experience that will last a lifetime is established.

However, this tension and intimidation isn't healthy! These feelings come when we feel like we're failing. We become fearful of another holiday turning into a shouting match, another year of financial restrictions, and another Christmas when our work schedules steal valuable family time. If we aren't careful, we can quickly enter into survival mode throughout the holiday season.

In the Old Testament, when King Hezekiah—Israel's leader—discovered that his then current sins would have a negative effect on his descendants, he didn't feel remorse. Instead, he selfishly thought, "There will be peace and security during my lifetime" (2 Kings 20:19). However, the beauty of the story is that despite his sins and the coming judgment, God's plan still moved forward. Even though Hezekiah's selfish actions hurt his children, it didn't condemn them. And even if we have experienced hurtful memories over the years or created hurtful memories for others, God is still a gracious redeemer. Because of His promise in Romans 8:28, we can have comfort: "We know that all things work together for the good of those who love God, who are called according to his purpose" (CSB). (**Further Reading:** Isaiah 39:5-40:11)

WHAT IS GOD TEACHING ME TO BE, THINK, OR DO TODAY...

DECEMBER 6
MY PATH IS ALREADY PAVED

You reveal the path of life to me; in Your presence is abundant joy; at Your right hand are eternal pleasures. (Psalm 16:11, HCSB)

Holidays are often associated with travel. People travel to see family, friends, or in search of a white Christmas. While it's easy to complain about heightened traffic on the streets or more people at the airports, we are blessed to be in the golden age of travel. How stressful must it have been for Mary to travel by donkey for hundreds of miles? She had no clue what the weather would be like, what obstacles she'd face, or the ETA of her route. Today, we Google an address and type it in our GPS. We don't blindly hope that we'll make it to our destination. Through the power of technology, experts have assured us of the right path to take.

Our faith lives work the same way. We have assurance of the right path to take because of the origins of Christmas. God had shown the path of obedience to His people throughout the Old Testament, but for generations they had failed to walk it faithfully. Isaiah even implored them to "wake up, wake up" (Isaiah 52:1), because they had fallen asleep on their journey—getting lost along the way.

However, the informed hope of Christmas is that Jesus provided a path through His own life. Jesus tells us in John 14:6: "I am the way, the truth, and the life. No one comes to the Father except through me" (HCSB). Spiritually, we are in the golden age of finding our path to God because Jesus has cleared it for us. He walked the path Himself, giving us turn by turn directions. We can trust that His expertise is greater than our personal experience. Let our prayer during and after this season be that our path singularly follows the direction of Christ. (**Further Reading:** Isaiah 52:1-12)

WHAT IS GOD TEACHING ME TO BE, THINK, OR DO TODAY...

DECEMBER 7
A BROKEN WORLD IN NEED

He will wipe away every tear from their eyes. Death will be no more; grief, crying, and pain will be no more, because the previous things have passed away. (Revelation 21:4, CSB)

When we zoom out from our personal lives and view the world at large, Christmas might be seen as a societal band-aid that has been used to cover up our problems. Cities, businesses, and neighborhoods are decorated with lights and trees, all while there is peppermint-scent flowing in the air. People attempt to be a little nicer by spreading holiday cheer, but as soon as the calendar turns, the world appears to be just as broken as ever.

God's people have always lived in the middle of a broken world. We know turmoil, distress, tears, and pain; it's a part of the human experience. We suffer the cultural consequences of walking in sin and turning our backs on God. However, we can take hope in the fact that brokenness is not final.

Paul tells us in Romans 8:18: "For I consider that the sufferings of this present time are not worth comparing with the glory that is going to be revealed to us. For the creation eagerly waits with anticipation for God's sons to be revealed" (HCSB). God promised that one day we will live in a new world that is free from brokenness, free from hurt, and free from the sin that causes us to stumble. This reality will not be a seasonal band-aid to simply cover earth's problems for a time. Instead, our world will be fully restored by an eternal God. My prayer is for us to be grounded in the promise of God's renewal so that we don't have to be anxious about all of the problems in our world today. This promise empowers us to live in the freedom of His grace! (**Further Reading:** Isaiah 61:1-4)

WHAT IS GOD TEACHING ME TO BE, THINK, OR DO TODAY...

DECEMBER 8
CRYING OUT TO MY HEAVENLY FATHER

Lord, hear my prayer; let my cry for help come before You. (Psalm 102:1, HCSB)

Arguably the most joyful group of people during the Christmas season are kids. It could be a child, grandchild, sibling, niece, nephew, or a friend's toddler; kids have a way of bringing joy and fresh eyes to the simplest beauties of the holidays. Have you ever noticed the extreme joy that spreads across a child's face when looking at Christmas lights?

Kids not only give us lessons on enjoying the beauty of life, but they also teach us where to turn when life gets hard. When a child is in danger, lost, or hurt, their natural reaction is to cry out for their father or mother. They cry out to be rescued, to be comforted, and to find healing in the arms of their parents.. As we get older, we somehow forget that we have the same invitation to cry out to our heavenly Father, and we can find ourselves never calling on His name.

During His life, Jesus provided us countless examples when it comes to crying out to our Father in heaven. We see one example in John 11:41-42: "Father, I thank You that You heard me. I know that You always hear me" (HCSB). What *father* do you cry out to for rescue, comfort, and healing? What *father* do you turn to for guidance in your life? Too often we cry out to the false fathers of self-help, addiction, and survival instead of our Father in heaven. Our identity and our future are dependent on who we look to as our father. We don't have to live independently; we can experience deep dependence on our heavenly Father who loves us.

Further Reading: Galatians 3:27-4:7

WHAT IS GOD TEACHING ME TO BE, THINK, OR DO TODAY...

DECEMBER 9
THE PAST IS RESTORED

Now faith is the reality of what is hoped for, the proof of what is not seen. For by this our ancestors were approved. (Hebrews 11:1-2, CSB)

For humanity, the Advent season is all about what is *coming*; for God, it's all about what He is *doing*. We cry out to God because we know that He is the only one who can truly fix the brokenness of our world. But, to truly understand how God fixes our world, we must take time during this season to reflect on His past, present, and future work.

The Old Testament is filled with stories about generations that were full of potential and full of God's blessing. But they all fell on their faces by allowing sin to trip them up. Regardless of how high they climbed, one after another fell short of perfection, failed to keep God's law, and didn't stay faithful to His commands. So what hope did the generations of God's people have despite the fact that they had sinned and turned their backs on God? What hope did Abraham, Moses, David, Esther, Isaiah, and Jeremiah have? Each one had Godly moments during their life, but they all were still sinners who died hundreds of years before Jesus was born.

Christmas is not just for us, but for those who came before. Despite their falling short of perfection, these generations that came before Jesus believed in a God that would provide "the reality of what is hoped for." They trusted a God who would not abandon His people, but would provide the means for salvation. This season should prompt us to pray prayers of thanksgiving for the examples we have in the Old Testament of the men and women who lived by radical faith for a Savior that had yet to come and for a God who never forgets His people. (**Further Reading:** 1 Thessalonians 4:13-18)

WHAT IS GOD TEACHING ME TO BE, THINK, OR DO TODAY...

DECEMBER 10
THE PRESENT IS AT PEACE

"Haven't I commanded you: be strong and courageous? Do not be afraid or discouraged, for the Lord your God is with you wherever you go." (Joshua 1:9, HCSB)

Have you noticed that holiday trends progress much slower than trends during the rest of the year? For example, breakthroughs in Christmas decorations are rare, holiday fashion looks the same every year, and new cultural trends are non-existent as lasting traditions prevail. Even church services usually lead people in the same traditional songs and the preaching focuses on the Christmas Story. It's hard to disrupt the traditions of a holiday that, for many, is about reliving old memories and celebrating the past.

Sadly, our spiritual lives can look very similar. Many know what Jesus did on the cross 2,000 years ago and celebrate that past. Meanwhile, they still worry about the present and don't dare move into the future. Christians seemingly fall into the trap of focusing on the good ol' days—when the world wasn't so bad and their hardships weren't so intense. However, Jesus never intended for us to avoid the present and even offered us comfort for it: "Peace I leave with you. My peace I give to you. I do not give to you as the world gives. Don't let your heart be troubled or fearful" (John 14:27, CSB).

Jesus is with you today, which means you don't have to be frustrated, stressed, or burdened with the outlook of the world. You are free to live in His peace. Paul tells us that we don't know when our future in heaven will come, so we should spend our time now building each other up and encouraging one another (1 Thessalonians 5:10-11). I pray that the peace of Jesus Christ, not just for the future, but for today, falls over you and empowers you to live for Him. (**Further Reading:** 1 Thessalonians 5:1-11)

WHAT IS GOD TEACHING ME TO BE, THINK, OR DO TODAY...

DECEMBER 11
THE FUTURE IS GUARANTEED

"For I know the plans I have for you"—this is the Lord's declaration—*"plans for your well-being, not for disaster, to give you a future and a hope."* (Jeremiah 29:11, CSB)

A favorite pastime for many people during the holiday season is watching Christmas movies. They have distinct features that seem to set them apart from all others: a narrow timeline, a light-hearted plot, similar character types, and most importantly, they always have a happy ending. From *It's a Wonderful Life* to *The Grinch* to *Charlie Brown* and *Elf*, a happy ending is a staple for any good Christmas movie. Despite the similar format, multiple viewing sessions, and already knowing the ending, people watch the same movies every Christmas season.

The Bible is no different! The happy ending is right in the text. We can read it over and over again, but the same truth continues to resonate loudly. Jesus is on His throne today, and for all eternity! The future of believers is secure because Jesus came to earth, lived a perfect life, died on the cross in our place, and overcame death when He rose from the grave.

It's almost like we are living in the middle of a Christmas movie: there will be laughs and moments of joy, but there will also be opposition and hard times. However, just like the ending of those classic movies, the story of our lives will end happily with our Lord. Let us pray for any stress and anxiety to be put to death as we rest on the truth that Jesus has secured our eternal destination.

Further Reading: 1 Corinthians 15:20-28

WHAT IS GOD TEACHING ME TO BE, THINK, OR DO TODAY...

DECEMBER 12
BY THE SAVIOR THAT REDEEMS

In Him we have redemption through His blood, the forgiveness of our trespasses, according to the riches of His grace that He richly poured out on us with all wisdom and understanding. (Ephesians 1:7-8, CSB)

The halfway point is a big deal in all of life's major milestones: college education, a big project, halftime of a sports game, reading a book, and even counting down the days to a big event. As we come to the halfway point of the Advent season, let's look at the event that cut history in half.

We are told in Acts 3:24: "In addition, all the prophets who have spoken, from Samuel and those after him, have also foretold these days" (CSB). When the calendar went from BC to AD, the "last days" that the prophets had foretold began. Christmas cut history into two ages—the age of promise and the age of fulfillment. We don't know when Jesus will return, but we are living in the fulfillment of God's Kingdom because of Jesus' birth, death, and resurrection. The full consummation of that Kingdom has not yet been seen, but we are living in the second half of history, experiencing the redemption of mankind.

As we get closer to celebrating Jesus' birth this Christmas, may we meditate on the freedom of this fulfillment that we live in. God has already fulfilled His promise, and we can have confidence that we will continue to experience that fulfillment more fully. God, we thank you for sending a Savior who brought peace to the past, the present, and to our eternal future.

Further Reading: Colossians 1:15-20

WHAT IS GOD TEACHING ME TO BE, THINK, OR DO TODAY...

_____

_____

_____

_____

_____

_____

_____

_____

_____

_____

_____

_____

_____

_____

_____

_____

_____

DECEMBER 13
A PRESENT POINTING TO A PRESENT

For God loved the world in this way: He gave His one and only Son, so that everyone who believes in Him will not perish but have eternal life. (John 3:16, HCSB)

The worst commercials during the holidays are the horrible car commercials that always include a wife unwrapping a small box with a car key inside. Obviously, the elaborate gift of receiving a car for Christmas is not a reality most people can relate to. However, maybe we can still relate to the imagery. Whenever that commercial-wife opens the box, her excitement doesn't stop with the key. The key is only exciting because it unlocks a brand new car, and with it, brand new possibilities.

A mistake that is easy to make is to think that the true gift of Christmas, Jesus in human flesh, stops there. The gift of Jesus didn't end with Him as a baby lying in a manger. His arrival was merely the key that unlocks access to the Kingdom of God.

John tells us to be thankful for the present of Jesus, who "became flesh, and dwelt among us" (John 1:14, HCSB). And that present ultimately opened up the possibility to experience the promise of "new heavens and a new earth, where righteousness dwells" (2 Peter 3:13, HCSB).

As we pray leading up to the days of Christmas, may we also pray for the eternal future that Jesus' birth makes possible to become our truest reality. We no longer have to endlessly and hopelessly strive to earn a place in God's story. Through the coming of Jesus, our place in His story is freely given.

Further Reading: 2 Peter 3:3-13

WHAT IS GOD TEACHING ME TO BE, THINK, OR DO TODAY...

DECEMBER 14
THE PRICE PAID BY THE KING

He emptied himself by assuming the form of a servant, taking on the likeness of humanity. And when he had come as a man, he humbled himself by becoming obedient to the point of death. (Philippians 2:7-8, HCSB)

Sacrifice is one of the biggest factors that separates highly successful people from others. That means sacrificing time, energy, resources, and even momentary enjoyments like food. If sacrifice was easy, everybody would do it! Even though we know that exercise, eating healthily, and saving our money will pay off in the end, it doesn't make it any easier at the moment. The Christmas season is undoubtedly the hardest time to make sacrifices. Many of us will overspend and overeat while spending time with family and friends because it's difficult to pay the price of sacrifice.

However, when we look at the Christmas story, we see that Jesus paid the ultimate price of sacrifice. Even though He was equal with God, He stepped down into humanity knowing it would cost His life. It is easy for us to focus on the coming of Jesus as the greatest gift mankind has ever received. Jesus' arrival also meant that He had to forsake His position of power, which ultimately led to human pain and suffering on earth. This wasn't a decision made on a whim or with uncertainty; it was an intentional decision by God the Father and His Son. Jesus knew the ugliness that laid before Him. He would be beaten, mocked, betrayed, and ultimately hung on a cross.

Let's pray and thank Jesus for making the decision to come to earth and pay the price for our sins. He endured pain along the way, and ultimately changed the course of history so that we can look forward to a future that we can enjoy. (**Further Reading:** Mark 14:60-65)

WHAT IS GOD TEACHING ME TO BE, THINK, OR DO TODAY...

DECEMBER 15
A PROMISE NOT FORGOTTEN

He who calls you is faithful; He will do it. (1 Thessalonians 5:24, CSB)

As joyous as Christmas can be, sometimes we just want it to end. It falls at the end of the calendar, and if it arrives at the end of a tough year, a natural longing is to get to a fresh start in the new year.

Imagine how the people of Israel felt during the time of the prophets. When Jeremiah was delivering words from God, they felt like their lives and kingdom were in ruins beyond repair. Even so, Jeremiah told them that God would keep His promises and restore a king on the throne. But in a time of despair, it must have been hard for them to believe. To make matters worse, after that time of that prophecy there was a period of 400 years of silence from God. For 400 years, God's chosen people experienced the temptation to simply give up and start something new. No more traditions, no more promises, and no more worship!

Likewise, we can fall into the same trap. We can buy into the lies that tell us that since things aren't as good as we would like, God must have forgotten us. When we can't see the immediate results that we desire, it's tempting to believe that He is no longer faithful when it comes to keeping His promises. Those thoughts are lies from the Devil, and each temptation should serve as a warning sign for us to run towards God instead of away from Him. Even in the darkest of times for the people of Israel, many of them remained faithful. They were confident that despite the hardships and silence, God would keep His promises. They had seen Him do it before and they knew that one day they would see it again.

My prayer is that because we know God faithfully keeps His word we all will trust the promises of God in seasons of plenty, but also in seasons of despair. (**Further Reading:** Jeremiah 33:14-17)

WHAT IS GOD TEACHING ME TO BE, THINK, OR DO TODAY...

DECEMBER 16
PEACE IN A SMALL PACKAGE

May the Lord of peace Himself give you peace always in every way. The Lord be with all of you. (2 Thessalonians 3:16, HCSB)

Christmas meals can be quite rambunctious. Often the greatest cause of the crazy energy is from the smallest people at the table. Nothing shakes up a family holiday like adding babies and toddlers into the mix. They may be small, but they are loud! They often bring more chaos and pandemonium than calm and peace.

Before Jesus came, the nation of Israel was in a perpetual state of chaos. They continuously found themselves looking for someone to calm the storm. The expectation was that peace throughout their land would come through one of their larger tribes like Judah, Manasseh, or Reuben. Those tribes held the most power and acted as the big brothers of Israel.

However, God promised that peace and prosperity for their land would come through the tribe of Benjamin, the smallest tribe. It would not come in the form of a superhero-like figure who fell from the sky. Instead, it would come on a quiet night in the form of a tiny infant.

God has a way of working in ways that we would never expect. We are often blind to His moving because it goes against our everyday logic. Israel was continuously told that the Savior was coming as a suffering servant from the smallest tribe, but they still missed Jesus when He arrived. Let's pray that God would give us eyes to see His words and promises play out every day in our lives.

Further Reading: Micah 5:2-5

WHAT IS GOD TEACHING ME TO BE, THINK, OR DO TODAY...

_____

_____

_____

_____

_____

_____

_____

_____

_____

_____

_____

_____

_____

_____

_____

DECEMBER 17
FINDING HIS FLOCK

For the Son of Man has come to seek and to save the lost. (Luke 19:10, HCSB)

One of the most difficult parts of the holidays is buying gifts for friends and family. Previously, people had to wait in long lines at the stores and brave crazy crowds. Now, we seem to simply order everything online, right from our phones. Despite its convenience, even this simplified shopping experience is not free from issues. Sometimes what gets delivered is not what we thought that we ordered, it doesn't arrive on time, or it is damaged upon arrival. It's safe to say that finding the perfect gift for a loved one is not usually an easy task.

Christmas is a reminder that just as we search for the perfect gift, God searches for His perfect people. I don't mean perfect in the sense that they haven't made any mistakes. We all do that daily! I'm talking about those who are sheep that are faithful to the shepherd and are made perfect by His salvation. Ezekiel paints a beautiful picture of God fulfilling His promise to not neglect or lose His people. Instead, He actively searches, protects, and saves them from the danger.

When God describes the nation of Israel as His "human flock of My pasture," (Ezekiel 34:31, HCB) He is ultimately describing us believers who are now the true children of God through Jesus. It's easy to feel lost and alone, just as Israel did. But the Bible gives us assurance that Jesus not only came down to "seek and save the lost," but also that God is still adding sheep to His flock today. I thank God that I am part of His flock and I desire to see His search continue to increase throughout our world today.

Further Reading: Ezekiel 34:11-31

WHAT IS GOD TEACHING ME TO BE, THINK, OR DO TODAY...

DECEMBER 18
A JEALOUS LOVE

Because the LORD is jealous for His reputation, you are never to bow down to another god. He is a jealous God. (Exodu 34:14, HCSB)

From a young age, we are taught to not be jealous of others. This life principle can be especially difficult to live out during Christmas. Kids may get jealous of a friends' present, teenagers may get jealous of other couples' relationships, and as adults, we may get jealous of other people's lives. In its most basic sense, jealousy isn't a bad thing. How we respond can be, though.

The Old Testament continuously describes God as jealous, but what does that mean? Jealousy in the Bible was used to describe God's intolerance of unfaithfulness and idolatry. Basically, He wanted His people to be faithful to Him as He was faithful to them. This jealousy of God is beautiful because it shows God's ultimate heart for His people. If you read through the Old Testament, it is filled with story after story about God's people betraying Him and turning to the wrong places for fulfillment. Today, we are all guilty of doing the exact same thing. We often try to find fulfillment and meaning in our jobs, our marriage, our kids, our stuff, and the list goes on and on. But despite our failures, God is still jealous for us. He is still pursuing us, ready to restore us when we turn back to Him.

It can be easy to get lost in the distractions of the Christmas season. Let's pray for strength to focus on being faithful to God who jealously loves us and wants our affection turned toward Him—not toward the garbage of the world.

Further Reading: Zechariah 8:1-8

WHAT IS GOD TEACHING ME TO BE, THINK, OR DO TODAY...

DECEMBER 19
HISTORY NOT FORGOTTEN

Who is a God like you, forgiving iniquity and passing over rebellion for the remnant of His inheritance? He does not hold on to His anger forever because He delights in faithful love. He will again have compassion on us; He will vanquish our iniquities. You will cast all our sins into the depths of the sea. (Micah 7:18-19, HCSB)

One of the most popular Christmas movies is *The Grinch*. This timeless classic seems to be so popular because it has an amazing character arc of redemption. As people, we love to see the angry, mean Grinch with a small heart turn into a joyful, giving hero with a heart so big that it breaks the scale. But, the redemption tale loses its significance if you don't first see how harsh the Grinch's origins were.

Matthew begins his Gospel story about Jesus with a genealogy of the family line who came before him. If you spend time going through those names and studying their lives, you will see story upon story about failure and sin. God even directed Matthew to highlight David's sin in the writing of the genealogy by not naming his wife Bathsheba, but instead referring to her as Uriah's wife. David's greatest sin was committing adultery and murder. Instead of God sweeping it under the rug and forgetting about it, it is cemented in the genealogy of the Savior of the world.

Why would God choose to remind us of all the brokenness that comes from Jesus' family line? He reminds us so that we can appreciate His grace and salvation even more! When God forgives our sins, we are no longer bound to their consequences. However, on this side of heaven the scars still show. Instead of trying to bury them and forget, we can rejoice that despite our flawed past, God still saves. Thank you, God, for giving us redemption through Jesus even though we don't deserve it. (**Further Reading**: Matthew 1:1-17)

WHAT IS GOD TEACHING ME TO BE, THINK, OR DO TODAY...

DECEMBER 20
PREPARING THE WAY

See, I am sending My messenger ahead of you; he will prepare your way. A voice of one crying out in the wilderness: Prepare the way for the Lord; make His paths straight! (Mark 1:3, CSB)

Have you ever woken up and not known what day it is? Maybe you felt completely unprepared for what was coming? Now imagine that happening on Christmas Day: no tree put up, no presents wrapped, and no plans with family. That would be a pretty disappointing day.

The day that forever changed history did not come without warning. Even though many did not listen, God was very intentional in making sure people would be prepared. Six months before Jesus was born, Elizabeth gave birth to His cousin, John the Baptist. God gave John the role of the messenger who would make sure His people weren't caught unprepared for the Savior who was coming.

John not only preceded Jesus in birth, but later in life, He preceded Jesus' ministry. The Holy Spirit filled John and equipped Him with power to prepare those around him for the Good News of the Messiah's arrival. He warned them to repent so that their hearts were ready to receive something truly life changing.

Are you prepared for Jesus' arrival on a daily basis? Furthermore, are you helping to prepare others? Christmas is the time that you can reflect on where you truly are with God. Is your life surrendered? Is your path straight toward Him or turned toward things that don't matter? And for those around us, are you actively using this season as an opportunity to share the Gospel? Let your prayers be for a heart of preparation, in your own life and in those who are around you.

Further Reading: Luke 1:5-25

WHAT IS GOD TEACHING ME TO BE, THINK, OR DO TODAY...

DECEMBER 21
HE IS NEAR

The Lord is near all who call out to Him, all who call out to Him with integrity. (Psalm 145:18, HCSB)

The nearness of something is a matter of perspective. Some people get excited when Thanksgiving is over because it means Christmas is *almost here*; others don't start thinking about it until they get off work for the week.

In Jesus' birth story, as soon as Mary was told that she would bring baby Jesus into the world, it probably instantly felt like He was near. The utter shock during her initial reaction surely must have caused her heart to sink and her jaw to drop as she wondered how something so impossible could happen. But God delivered the news to Mary through an undeniable messenger—the angel named Gabriel. Mary quickly set aside her doubt and accepted what God was doing. He was bringing the Savior of the world, into the world, through her. The time was growing near, and instead of running away, Mary leaned in.

Her response in Luke's account was not "No thank you," but rather, "I am the Lord's servant" (Luke 1:38). Now that's a powerful statement from a scared teenage girl who God called to change history forever…"I am the Lord's servant."

As you reflect on how near the Lord is this holiday season, what will your response be? Will you deny it? Will you run from it? Will you get distracted? Or will you embrace your role in God's plan? My prayer is that as the Advent calendar winds down, you develop a willingness to be God's servant and be used for His will.

Further Reading: Luke 1:26-38

WHAT IS GOD TEACHING ME TO BE, THINK, OR DO TODAY...

DECEMBER 22
WE SHOULD FEAR

In the fear of the Lord one has strong confidence and his children have a refuge. (Proverbs 14:26, HCSB)

Whenever a big day approaches, a natural emotion that comes along with it is fear. We might fear that we forgot something important, that things won't go according to plan, that someone might disappoint us, or even that we will fail in some way. Many approach Christmas with fear. It might surprise you to know that I believe we should have fear during Christmas, but not with the type of fear you might be thinking about.

While Mary prepared herself for Jesus to come, she visited her cousin, Elizabeth, and found encouragement through her. One of the most powerful moments of their interaction was when Mary broke out into a praise break for the Lord.

Here's what Luke said about her recognition of just how great God actually is: "His mercy is from generation to generation on those who fear Him" (Luke 1:50, HCSB). Mary understood how powerful God was and never thought lightly of that truth. She constantly reflected on how unworthy she was in comparison to God's greatness. As she approached Jesus' momentous birth, the magnitude of it caused her to humble herself before God. She submitted herself to His service in reverent fear of Him, knowing that He was in control.

When Christmas draws close, it should cause us to reflect on the magnitude of our God and how undeserving we are of His affection. We should fear Him because of how sinful, broken, and powerless we are in comparison to how holy, perfect, and powerful He is. Let us pray for such a grand picture of God—the kind we see throughout the Bible—that it stirs healthy fear in our hearts and causes us to run to Him for refuge. (**Further Reading:** Luke 1:39-56)

WHAT IS GOD TEACHING ME TO BE, THINK, OR DO TODAY...

DECEMBER 23
THE CHILD IS BORN

Therefore, the Lord Himself will give you a sign: See, the virgin will conceive, have a son, and name Him Immanuel. (Isaiah 7:14, HCSB)

As the end of Advent draws near, let's reflect on the meaning of Christ's coming to earth. It is so much more than a fairy tale or story about a made-up man in a red suit who achieves something in one night that isn't physically possible. Rather, Jesus' birth is a historic event when the supernatural and eternal collided with the natural and temporal.

A baby that was born more than 2,000 years ago changed the course of human history. How? Look no further than His name—Immanuel, God with us. The beauty of the Advent season is that God came down to be with us. It was no longer about us failing, growing further apart from God, searching for meaning in meaningless places, or our enslavement to past sins and mistakes. God came to erase all of that for us.

It is only by the presence of someone immortal and eternal that our relationship with our Creator can be restored. So, when we celebrate the birth of Jesus, it's not because of an unforeseen hope that is yet to come. It's because of the holy presence of our God that we as mankind did nothing to deserve. Let's pray today and invite God to encounter us with His humanity-changing presence in a deeper way than ever before, and let us humble ourselves before Him so that He can continue to transform our lives to be more like Him.

Further Reading: Matthew 1:18-25

WHAT IS GOD TEACHING ME TO BE, THINK, OR DO TODAY...

DECEMBER 24
HEAVEN IS HERE

"If I am not doing My Father's works, don't believe Me. But if I am doing them and you don't believe Me, believe the works. This way you will know and understand that the Father is in Me and I in the Father." (John 10:37-38, HCSB)

Christmas Eve is traditionally the last day of Advent. It's the time when we joyfully look to the birth of Jesus Christ as the high point and ending of this season of anticipation. It is filled with joy because of all of the hardships, prophecies, and waiting for Jesus. The Savior came to rescue us from death and create something new for all eternity. Tomorrow, on Christmas day, we will read the traditional Christmas story as told by Luke which gives the historical account of this momentous event. But for today, let's reflect on the spiritual reality of this time.

Of all the Gospel writers, John was the least concerned with being a meticulous historian. He was more of the abstract-theologian type. Instead of painting a picture that's easy to visualize, he provided us with a spiritual image that almost overwhelms our senses. In John 1:1-3, he tells us: "In the beginning was the Word, and the Word was with God, and the Word was God. He was with God in the beginning. All things were created through Him, and apart from Him not one thing was created that has been created" (HCSB).

Often, we naturally view the start of Jesus' journey at Christmas with His earthly birth. However, John and many writers throughout the New Testament challenge us to expand our spiritual view and see how Jesus has been present and active throughout all of existence. He was involved in creation, involved in choosing Israel as God's chosen people, involved in getting them back on track, and involved in speaking through the prophets. Furthermore, after witnessing the continual drifting of His sheep, He brought heaven, Himself, down to us. God, we thank you for forsaking your power and stepping down to earth for us. You brought a light that pushed back darkness and opened up the door to heaven. (**Further Reading:** John 1:1-18)

WHAT IS GOD TEACHING ME TO BE, THINK, OR DO TODAY...

_____

_____

_____

_____

_____

_____

_____

_____

_____

_____

_____

_____

_____

_____

_____

_____

_____

DECEMBER 25
CHRISTMAS BRINGS CHEER

Be glad in the Lord and rejoice, you righteous ones; shout for joy, all you upright in heart. (Psalm 32:11, HCSB)

On December 19, 1843, Charles Dickens published the now classic story called *A Christmas Carol*. Since that day, it has been read, watched, and told countless times. In fact, there are over 135 variations of that timeless story. Some stories like this one never seem to grow old or tiresome, and some even contain truth that transcends time and culture.

No story contains that timeless truth like the Bible. Arguably, no story in all of the Bible is more widely circulated and known than Jesus' birth. Many who grew up in church have heard this story more times than they can remember. They have seen the plays, heard the sermons, re-enacted the nativity scene on their front lawns, and can probably recall all of the details.

As we read this story again this Christmas, the challenge is to not take its significance for granted. It's not just a classic story that simply brings up fond memories or entertains us during the Christmas season. Rather, it's the beginning of the greatest life the world has ever seen. Jesus has not only shaped all of history, but He is also shaping our present reality and future eternity.

When we read, listen to, and recall the birth of Jesus this Christmas, our reaction should be the same as the shepherds on that first Christmas night. They praised God and shouted with joy because they were lost, but Jesus' arrival gave them the opportunity to be found. Let's praise God with great cheer this Christmas for coming to us and changing everything!

Further Reading: Luke 2:1-20

WHAT IS GOD TEACHING ME TO BE, THINK, OR DO TODAY...

NOTES

Chapter 1

1. Canfield, Jack, et al. *Chicken Soup for the Soul : It's Christmas! : 101 Joyful Stories about the Love, Fun, and Wonder of the Holidays.* Cos Cob, Ct, Chicken Soup For The Soul Publishing, 2013.
2. "In the Fullness of Time by David Holwerda." *Ligonier Ministries*, www.ligonier.org/learn/articles/fullness-time/.
3. "Look Who's Here." *Christian Motivations*, christianmotivations.weebly.com/christian-motivations-blog/look-whos-here. Accessed 30 Aug. 2021.

Chapter 2

1. "PressReader.com - Digital Newspaper & Magazine Subscriptions." *Www.pressreader.com*, www.pressreader.com/usa/readers-digest/20190101/282132112418119. Accessed 30 Aug. 2021.
2. "A Most Violent Year: The World into Which Jesus Was Born." *ABC News*, 16 Dec. 2015, www.abc.net.au/religion/a-most-violent-year-the-world-into-which-jesus-was-born/10097496.
3. "Thomas Oliphant – Deck the Halls." *Genius.com*, genius.com/Thomas-oliphant-deck-the-halls-lyrics. Accessed 9 July 2021.
4. Chapman, Morris, and Southern Baptist Convention. Pastors' Conference. *Jesus, Author and Finisher*, pg. 153. Nashville, Tenn., Broadman Press, 1987.
5. "Hate Christmas? There's a 'Rage Room' to Let out Holiday Stress." *www.cbsnews.com*, www.cbsnews.com/news/christmas-rudolph-rage-room-london-holidays/. Accessed 9

July 2021.

6. Speas, Ralph. *How to Deal with How You Feel*. Nashville, Tenn., Broadman Press, 1980.

7. Chapman, Morris, and Southern Baptist Convention. Pastors' Conference. *Jesus, Author and Finisher*, pg. 154-155. Nashville, Tenn., Broadman Press, 1987.

Chapter 3

1. Swindoll, Charles R. *Insights on Romans*. Grand Rapids, Mich., Zondervan, 2010.

2. Twain, Mark. *Following the Equator*. Oxford, Oxon, John Beaufoy Publishing, Ltd, 2017.

3. The Hound of Heaven by Francis Thompson. Nicholson & Lee, Eds. 1917. The Oxford Book of English Mystical Verse." *www.bartleby.com*, www.bartleby.com/236/239. html. Accessed 21 July 2021.

4. "Amazing Grace Lyrics." *Www.lyrics.com*, www.lyrics.com/lyric/30558307/Hymns/Amazing+Grace. Accessed 21 July 2021.

Chapter 4

1. "The Men Who Hate Christmas so Much They Want to Destroy It." *MEL Magazine*, 19 Dec. 2018, melmagazine. com/en-us/story/the-men-who-hate-christmas-so-much-they-want-to-destroy-it. Accessed 22 July 2021.

2. Swindoll, Charles R. *Insights on Romans*. Grand Rapids, Mich., Zondervan, 2010.

3. "55 Old Testament Prophecies about Jesus | Jesus Film Project." *www.jesusfilm.org*, www.jesusfilm.org/blog-and-stories/old-testament-prophecies.html.

Chapter 5

1. "Christmas Changes Everything - Josh Wilson." *SongLyrics. com*, www.songlyrics.com/josh-wilson/christmas-changes-everything-lyrics/. Accessed 18 Aug. 2021.
2. "Fifty Years Later, 'Peace Child' Tribe Still Following Christ." *Mission Network News*, www.mnnonline.org/news/fifty-years-later-peace-child-tribe-still-following-christ. Accessed 18 Aug. 2021.
3. "Joy to the World Lyrics | Christmas Carols." *www. lyricsforchristmas.com*, www.lyricsforchristmas.com/christmas-carols/joy-to-the-world/. Accessed 18 Aug. 2021.
4. H Edwin Young. *Been There. Done That. Now What? : The Meaning of Life May Surprise You*. Nashville, Tenn., Broadman & Holman Publishers, 1994.
5. Davidman, Joy. *Smoke on the Mountain : An Interpretation of the Ten Commandments*. Philadelphia, Westminster Press, 1985.
6. "All Things in Jesus." *Hymnary.org*, hymnary.org/text/friends_all_around_us_are_trying_to_find. Accessed 18 Aug. 2021.
7. Warren, Rick. *The Purpose of Christmas*. New York, Howard Books, 2018.
8. "Oh, Holy Night." *Hymnary.org*, hymnary.org/text/o_holy_night_the_stars_are_brightly_shin. Accessed 18 Aug. 2021.

Chapter 6

1. "Go, Tell It on the Mountain." *Hymnary.org*, hymnary.org/text/while_shepherds_kept_their_watching. Accessed 26 Aug. 2021.

2. Stier, Greg. "5 Simple Ways to Share Christ This Christmas." *ChurchLeaders*, 10 Dec. 2018, churchleaders. com/youth/youth-leaders-articles/314893-5-simple-ways-share-christ-christmas-greg-stier.html. Accessed 26 Aug. 2021.

Advent Devotional

1. "Preparing to Receive Christ: Looking for the Consolation of Israel." *Desiring God*, 21 Dec. 1986, www.desiringgod. org/messages/preparing-to-receive-christ-looking-for-the-consolation-of-israel. Accessed 28 Aug. 2021.

ADDITIONAL RESOURCES

To access free sermon outlines and graphics for the Christmas Comes sermon series visit **christmascomesbook.com.**

To hear the most recent messages from Pastor Jackie visit **crosschurchcares.com/surprise/sermons.**

To purchase Jackie's leadership book *Bad Bosses,* visit **badbossesbook.com.**

And to inquire about scheduling Pastor Jackie for a speaking engagement for your church or team email **info@ crosschurchcares.com.**

Made in the USA
Las Vegas, NV
15 October 2021